"My passion of serving Christ for a lifetime is the legacy I want to leave to future generations, and I'm sure you do too. This book will make the 'how's' easy to understand and give you a plan on how to do it. *Handoff* is well written and very helpful—you need to read it!"

Dr. Tim LaHaye, Author, Minister, Educator
Co-author of the Left Behind series

"So many young people grow up feeling no one showed them the rule book to succeed in finding purpose and a fulfilling life. They feel they have to win the lottery to succeed. Jeff has provided all of us adults with great content written in a powerful way to impact the next generation, creating leaders who can succeed, no matter the challenges ahead."

Steve Arterburn, Founder, New Life Ministries

"*Handoff* is a treasure chest full of golden nuggets revealing not only how to reach out and share our lives with those hurting around us, but *give* our lives to them…. I trust *Handoff* will spur each reader on to step up to the plate—to be the ones who inspire and lead the younger people in our country today."

Joe White, President, Kanakuk/Kanakomo Sports Kamps

"Jeff Myers shows how each of us can be foot soldiers to win the battle for the next generation. It's time to secure our legacy. Absorb this book. Act on what you learn. It's a once in a lifetime cause."

Dr. David Noebel, President, Summit Ministries

"There's no greater challenge in contemporary society than to pass on to the next generation the mission and vision of following Jesus Christ. It does not happen by accident, but it must be intentional and consistent. Dr. Jeff Myers does it again in telling us both why and how to carry out this crucial task. Read this book! You won't be able to look at your life and ministry the same again."

Dr. Bill Brown, President, Cedarville University

"Some people bring competence to the challenges they take on; others bring passion. But Jeff Myers always brings both. And when he applies them to a topic as important as passing our faith on to the next generation, you've got a very worthwhile read."

Joel Belz, Founder and Columnist, World Magazine

"When I first met Jeff Myers a few months ago, he casually mentioned *Handoff* and gave me a pre-publication copy. I began reading but I must admit I had very modest expectations. WOW! This book is both very alarming and hopeful. *Handoff* will forever change the way you view a young person."

Stu Epperson, Chairman, Salem Communications Corporation

"If Dr. Myers' call to train and engage one million new mentors becomes reality we will experience a tremendous impact across the nation with families, communities and classrooms. Read *Handoff*, learn and engage, and you'll know how to become a part of this life-giving movement."

Paul Stanley, International Vice-President of Navigators
Co-author of Connecting: The Mentoring Relationships
You Need to Succeed in Life

"*Handoff* is a desperately needed and superbly written resource. It gives hope and practical advice on how to transform self-absorbed young people into the godly Christian, business and political leaders our country needs."

Ken Sande, President, Peacemaker Ministries

"This issue of preparing the next generation is crucial, and this book is practical. Jeff has provided words that inspire and equip adults to invest their lives in students. Mentoring, coaching and discipleship are worth giving your life to—which is what I plan to do. This book is a sort of job description. Every one of us can do it."

Dr. Tim Elmore, President, Growing Leaders International

"Jesus impacted the history of the world in just three short years by mentoring a few disciples, knowing that the future depended upon the few rather than upon the masses. Jeff Myers draws the reader into the meaningful and rewarding ministry of mentoring in his fascinating book, *Handoff*. If you have any doubts about using your influence to help shape young leaders for the next generation, this book will dispel your doubts and inspire you to pursue mentoring wholeheartedly!"

Dr. Roger Glidewell, Founder and Executive Director
Global Youth Ministry

"Jeff Myers has captured the insight of the Bible as well as the testimony of history. Life is a relay race, and the character of one generation is measured by how it has handed the baton of a Kingdom worldview to the future sons of the Kingdom. As you read this book, let God convict, confirm and bring hope. It is not too late to relate what you have learned from your Heavenly Father!"

Dr. Paul Jehle, President, Plymouth Rock Foundation

I AM SO GRATEFUL
to Beth Impson for the editing and
encouragement, to the Woodsons for
believing in this project, to Danielle
who demonstrates excellent baton-passing
skills every day, to those dozens of people
who passed the baton of godly faithfulness
to me, and to my children who are warming up
for the race of life.

Handoff

The Only Way to

Win the Race of Life

Jeff Myers, Ph.D.

President
Passing the Baton International, Inc.
www.passingthebaton.org

1st printing: March 2008
2nd printing: June 2008
3rd printing: September 2008

Scripture quotations are from The Holy Bible, English Standard
Version®, copyright © 2001 by Crossway Bibles, a publishing ministry of
Good News Publishers. Used by permission. All rights reserved.

Cover design: Margie Travis Wertz, www.keenermarketing.net

ISBN-13: 978-0-9815049-0-2
ISBN-10: 0-9815049-0-6

1. Mentoring. 2. Discipleship—Christianity. 3. Leadership—Succession.

P.O. Box 7
Dayton, TN 37321
423-570-1000
www.handoffbook.com

What You'll Discover In These Pages:

Full Disclosure:
The Embarrassing Reason
I Had to Write This Book

I WISH I WOULD HAVE KNOWN TEN YEARS AGO WHAT I'M ABOUT TO SHARE WITH YOU. When I started teaching full-time ten years ago, I had the wrong idea about how to influence the next generation. It's not that I didn't want to teach; teaching is the one thing I cannot *not* do. I love to synthesize complicated information into livable principles, I crave the "ah-ha" look on young faces and I'm thrilled when my students choose the good and the true.

My mistake was to assume that what happened in the classroom was my greatest source of influence. I put everything I had into my lectures and then rushed off to work on books or speeches.

I was getting a lot of strokes for this. My students were impressed with all the places I had been and people I had met. They begged for stories and I obliged.

And the opportunities continued to expand. About 10,000 people attended my workshops and speeches each year, then 30,000, then 80,000. I designed video-based study courses and published books to help folks master communication and leadership so they could make a difference.

But this whole time there was a tradition at our Bryan College commencement ceremony that really got to me. For many years graduates at our institution were given 15 seconds to say "thank you" to the professors who had helped them succeed. Some names came up over and over again. Never mine.

It's embarrassing to admit that I was irked by this. I'm a professional and I don't need that kind of recognition to feel good about my contribution, right? Still I couldn't shake the perception that influence in students' lives was strongly correlated with a personal investment of time.

I reflected back on the teachers who had made a difference in *my* life and realized that I was not like them. Whereas they invested personally in me, I always privileged the large, superficial kind of influence over the small, intensive kind. I was covering the globe but making very little impression on it.

Over the next few years I began looking for opportunities to genuinely influence students. I visited with them in the halls, I met them for lunch, and when they asked for counsel, I found time to get together.

And you know what? I realized that my fears—that I wouldn't be adequate, that I would lose my independence, that I would be overwhelmed, that I would be playing favorites—were unfounded. I learned to show caring without cultivating an over-dependence. I learned to converse and not just give lectures.

In the process, I discovered a whole new source of blessing. I mentored many wonderful young people. My wife and I hosted students in our home and had a delightful time. I began looking forward to walking with my students.

My creed used to be, "Reach as many people as you can, as quickly as you can." It's different now. I won't share the whole thing with you, but here are some parts of it:

- Life is a relay. I only win when I pass the baton to those who come after me—first to my children and then to others through an expanding sphere of influence.
- I teach what I know, but I reproduce who I am. I seek genuine influence, not as a burden to carry but as a gift to give away.
- I constantly kindle my own fire of inquisitiveness. I am a teachable teacher.
- I do not recoil when confronted with the hardness of life. Rather, I surrender the outcome to God and look forward to how He will bring redemption.

That's what this book is all about. As you read you'll also discover:

- The habits and strategies of those who win the race of life.
- What we can learn from a six hundred year old Muslim invader about ensuring our country's greatness.
- Why the next generation is so hard to reach, and how their silence can turn deadly.
- What I learned from my cowboy grandpa about giving meaning to both painful and joyful experiences.
- What a sled dog taught me about living with joy and purpose.
- Steps a dictatorial college administrator took to turn students into leaders.
- Why Mary Poppins was wrong—and why it is good to not strive for perfection.
- How to communicate truth to those who do not want to hear it.
- The right questions to ask to unleash a person's true talent.

- A strong-hearted response to failure and decadence.
- A lesson from a losing Tanzanian runner about the most important thing in winning the race of life.

I've shared these things with audiences for many years now, and two questions always come up repeatedly: "Can we possibly succeed in passing the baton?" and "Will it make a difference if we do?"

Frankly, I don't have all the answers, but I do know that we're rounding the last curve in the track. The next generation glances our way in hope and expectation, hand outstretched, poised to burst into the sprint of life.

In the coming decades folks will assess our generation based on how we passed the baton with so much at stake. What will our generation's story be?

Lessons from Civilizations Past

"The time for silence is past. The time to speak has come."

Martin Luther

THE 2004 U.S. WOMEN'S 4 X 100 RELAY TEAM, NOW TAINTED BY SCANDAL, PERFORMED IMPRESSIVELY IN THE SEMI-FINALS OF THE 2004 ATHENS OLYMPICS. Commentators confidently predicted that the gold medal was assured.

In the finals Marion Jones completed the second leg, while teammate Lauryn Williams bolted from her starting position, thrust her arm back, and anticipated the thump of the baton being pressed into her hand.

She never felt it.

Said Jones, "I just couldn't get the baton to Lauryn . . . I kept yelling, 'wait, stop, hold up' but after running 100 meters I was out of breath and I don't know if she could hear me."

By the time Williams understood the situation, it was too late. She had crossed out of the exchange zone. As long as they were in that zone, they could have even dropped the baton and picked it up to finish the race. But once they passed out of that zone without the baton having been passed, they were disqualified according to Olympic rules.

The women's relay team had entered the Olympics with great promise, but one missed baton pass dashed all hopes for a gold medal.

Graceful baton passes can make or break a relay team. Most teams succeed most of the time. Even if they don't, there's usually another race.

In the race of life, though, there is only one chance to make the pass, and the plain fact is that this generation is in danger of missing it.

George Barna, the researcher whose studies of church people offer tremendous insight into what the future holds, recently sounded the alarm:

Who are the successors we are preparing to stand on our shoulders and build on the foundations we have laid—as our fathers did with us? . . . it's not happening.[1]

A quick review of the facts shows this to be disturbingly true:

- *The baton is not being passed in business.* The *Harvard Business Review* reports that "The CEO succession process is broken in North America and is no better in many other parts of the world."[2] Five hundred of the largest companies can expect to lose 50 percent of their senior management by 2010 and 40% of companies don't have a leadership succession plan.[3]

- *The baton is not being passed in government. Governing* magazine reports that as baby boomers retire, the knowledge and experience necessary to conduct government is going out the door with them.[4] Warns Secretary of Labor Elaine Chao, "The looming retirement of so many baby boomers is a seismic event that will affect our workforce in profound ways."[5] As an example, MIT professor David DeLong says that NASA would have to start from scratch to conduct a moon landing because those on the original team have all retired or passed away.[6]

- *The baton is not being passed in the church.* The number of adults who do not attend church in America has nearly doubled since 1991, and only 51% of Protestant pastors and just 8% of Protestant parishioners possess a biblical worldview.[7]

- *The baton is not being passed in the home.* According to George Barna, "Fewer than one-twentieth of churched households ever worship God outside of a church service or have any type of regular Bible study or devotional time together during a typical week."[8]

In every significant social institution—the church, the government, commerce and the family—the current generation of leaders is failing to pass the baton of leadership to the next generation.

This crisis is so severe that today's leaders, the baby boom generation, are coming under withering criticism. Commentator Dennis Prager suggests that "The baby boomer generation needs to apologize to America, especially its young generation, for many sins."[9]

Sociologists acknowledge that the baby boom generation was different than previous generations in that it embraced radically different values than preceding generations. Mary Farrar explains in her book *Choices*:

> If you are a baby boomer, you are part of a generation that has chosen the dysfunctional path. Three and a half decades ago we baby boomers made a decision not to listen to God anymore. We threw out Scripture and rebelled against its authority. We determined that there are no absolutes, no timeless right or wrong. We

concluded that "right" is whatever seems or feels right at the moment. And in so doing we refused to acknowledge what the world has known for centuries, that the absence of morality is the presence of immorality. That free sex, free choice, and free thought are never "free" when they are set free from the moral law of God.[10]

Of course, this is not the fault of the entire baby boom generation, or even any given member of it. Good and noble things have been done by baby boomers in every sphere of life. Yet because they are failing to pass the baton of godly faithfulness, Western Civilization is losing its influence as a beacon of Christian love, economic freedom, and democracy. Can the death of everything we hold dear be far behind?

The answer to that question depends on what each and every one of us do now.

What the Winners in the Race of Life Do Differently

"This is our moment
Here at the crossroads of time
We hope our children carry our dreams down the line
They are the vintage
What kind of life will they live?
Is this a curse or a blessing that we give?"
Billy Joel, "Two Thousand Years"

Referring to the current leadership succession crisis, David DeLong of MIT says, "The situation is scary. People don't know what to do. But we can't give up just because it looks hard."[11]

The next generation is our hope. Imagine Christian young people preparing to become political leaders, college professors, research scientists, and business owners. Think of what could happen if our children grew up to stand for truth and fight against evil and injustice.

Together we must do all we can to make it happen. It has been said that there are no passengers on the ship of life—only crew. Simply put, the winners in the race of life are those who successfully pass the baton of godly faithfulness to the next generation.

This must be our cause. We must each make a successful pass to our loved ones, and then to those in our neighborhoods, churches and schools.

If we succeed, we'll see the next generation leap explosively toward great deeds, purpose, and service. Fail, and we leave them flailing, cynical, and aimless.

EVERYONE PASSES THE BATON

It's worth noting that we cannot *not* pass the baton to the next generation. Either we pass it purposefully or we fling it out of our casket just before they lower us into the ground. Everyone passes the baton: whether it is a strong pass or a weak one is up to each of us.

Intentionally passing the baton to the next generation is the single most important thing we must do now. If we get this right, everything else will take care of itself. If we don't, the lessons of history will be erased, the gains of the patriots will be negotiated away, the capital of the adventurous will be wasted on bread and circuses. The great historian Will Durant said, "From barbarism to civilization requires a century, from civilization to barbarism needs but a day."

If we could turn our baton-passing responsibility over to someone else, then this book would be unnecessary. But it is up to *all* of us, to each individual. Like it or not, we are either a part of the solution or we are part of the problem.

WHY THIS BOOK?

I'm writing this book because I not only want to be *in* the race of life. I want to *win*. I want to run hard and slap the baton into the hands of my children, my students, and the young people in my community. I want my last thoughts to be of immense pride as they explode down the track.

For a long time I thought I could accomplish this just by existing. I'm a teacher by trade, and teachers get lots of kudos for "investing in youth." Plus, I'm a dad, and my kids like me. Why shouldn't I just kick back?

Because that's not living. The only question history will ask of me, the One Important Question, is "What are you passing on?"

The universe is designed in such a way that passing the baton is the only way I can truly experience blessing, fullness, meaning, satisfaction, and joy in life. I may want to believe that serving myself leads to happiness, but my heart knows better. No matter how much stuff I buy, or what kind of house I live in, or where I travel, life only takes on meaning when I live for something bigger than myself.

This is a book about how to gracefully pass the baton to the next generation. It is a book about life, and as such, it is also about business, education, and parenting. I don't have any 39-

step plan, no miracle cure, just advice from one runner to another about the race of life.

This is a presumptuous book. I don't just want you to feel warm fuzzies toward other people. I want you to be seized by the gloriousness of slapping the baton firmly into the hands of your children and the young people in your church, neighborhood and community. I want you to leave it all on the field of life. I want you to inhale the pure oxygen of truth, get a second wind, and live inspirationally to the benefit of all those around you.

This is also a risky book. In it I claim that you'll only experience a meaningful life when you reach out to others. But that could hurt. Maybe no one ever reached out to you, so you're not sure what to do. Maybe you've tried to reach out and it didn't work. Maybe your heart has been broken.

I can relate to this fear, and it is painful. However, it is also irrelevant. Our choice is whether we pass the baton of godly faithfulness with purpose or without, intentionally or unintentionally, strongly or weakly.

The number one thing that could stop us is the battle between two sides of our nature, the giver and the taker. To win the race of life, we've got to feed the giver and starve the taker.

Let's take a look at how to do that next.

Feed the Giver, Starve the Taker

"One can give without loving, but one cannot love without giving."

Amy Carmichael

There's an old Tennessee story of a man who visited a farmer friend. As they sat on the porch rocking back and forth, two of the farmer's dogs got into a fight. Startled, the visitor asked, "Aren't you going to stop them?"

"Nah, they'll stop soon enough. They fight all the time."

"Which one wins?" asked the visitor.

"Whichever one I feed the most," the farmer replied.

With every action we either feed or starve the two competing sides of our nature, the giver side and the taker side. Our Inner Taker is the injured part of our soul. It makes withdrawals from the bank of life while only rarely making deposits. This side of us can never get enough. It consumes, consumes, consumes.

The Inner Giver appears in moments of selfless action. We give others the benefit of the doubt. We come up with ideas that make life better. This side must be intentionally cultivated and disciplined, but when it is, our lives become vibrant expressions of God's grace.

Think about the culture that influences young people every day. Which side of their natures is being fed? Which side of your own nature is being fed?

I'm told that the average American sees in the neighborhood of 1,600 commercial messages a day, from t-shirts to cereal boxes to billboards. Each message encourages us to consume more. Even in the midst of the September 11th crisis, Americans couldn't escape it. Government officials solemnly advised citizens that it would be good for the economy, and thus a patriotic duty, to go shopping.

Some of my youth-worker friends are concerned that by allowing kids to be overly-immersed in the entertainment and commercial culture we are feeding their Inner Takers. And because their Inner Givers won't grow unless intentionally cultivated, we have raised a generation whose primary identification is as consumers, not producers.

Those who give in to their Inner Taker ultimately live miserably. They don't build anything of enduring value, they don't leave others better off, they don't rescue the perishing. They suck the marrow out of life, and then they die.

Those who cultivate the Inner Giver, on the other hand, learn to build and deposit and grow. They gain favor with God and man. When difficulty chips away at them, it only reveals a deeper beauty. They are *blessed*.

Takers walk away from difficulties while givers take them as they come. Takers tolerate people, givers shape them. Takers grow more needy, givers more generous. Takers fill their houses with junk, givers fill their lives with memories.

You and I develop into givers or takers through the endless choices we make every day.

It's paradoxical isn't it? That meaning only comes to you when you impart meaning to others? That joy only floods your soul when you spread joy to others? That you are filled with blessing only to the degree that you bless others?

The good news—and it is *very* good news—is that it's never too late to begin starving your Inner Taker and feeding your Inner Giver. It starts with the next decision you make, and with how you answer the One Important Question: What are you passing on?

BEYOND MERE EXISTENCE

Of course, the issue for most people is not that dramatic. They're not Ebenezer Scrooge, but they're not Mother Teresa either. They aren't shriveled and bitter, but they sure aren't saintly. They just sort of exist.

Let's be honest. How many days do you submit to enormous drudgery just so you don't feel like a failure? It's the rat race, and as actress Lily Tomlin famously observed, "The trouble with the rat race is that even if you win, you're still a rat."

If it's a cause you're looking for, this is it. What can be more urgent than equipping the next generation to live heroically in a crisis world? This is a call to schools, churches, and youth-serving organizations, but it is also a call to *me*. To *you*.

In a relay race, the responsibility for passing the baton falls to the one who is carrying it, not to the one who is receiving it. That means that this is your lucky day. An entire generation is looking to you to lift their eyes to a higher goal— a life of character, friendship and community, a life that grows richer by giving rather than getting. And you *do* have something to give, even if you're disappointed with yourself. Your *mess* is your *message*.

THE ONLY THING I KNOW FOR SURE

Here's what I know for certain: the only way I can win the race of life is by ensuring that those who follow me have a better shot at winning. The training strategy you'll find here is very simple. It's unconventional, but it works. I've *seen* it work in the lives of thousands of young people and adults.

As a friend of mine here in Tennessee is fond of saying, "This ain't rocket surgery!" You don't have to be a leader. You don't have to be gifted. You just have to have a spirit that hungers for a more meaningful life.

Yet the forces of apathy and evil press in on every side, and they are not at all what you would expect.

Why the Next Generation is So Hard to Reach

"The sin of our times is the sin that believes in nothing,
cares for nothing, seeks to know nothing,
interferes with nothing, enjoys nothing, hates nothing,
finds purpose in nothing, lives for nothing, and
remains alive because there is nothing for which it will
die."

Dorothy Sayers

PSYCHIC NUMBING IS A TERM COINED BY ROBERT J. LIFTON in his book about Hiroshima survivors, *Death in Life.* By psychic numbing he means an emotional defense mechanism that injured people use to repress truth and ignore problems that are too great to solve.

People describe this generation as apathetic, but the true state of youth today is much more nuanced. They're actually psychically numb.

This generation of young adults lives in a time when disease, terrorism, and governmental instability are matters of fact. Today's youth do not remember, and cannot imagine, a world without violent gangs, AIDS, terrorism, genocide, and famine, and where such things are so publicly and vividly worried about.

Juxtaposed with these horrors is the ready access to amusement, both licit and illicit. With shopping and surfing available 24 hours a day young adults believe they can have whatever they want, whenever they want, however they want, and with whomever they want to have it. Nothing is more than a few clicks away.

Here's the paradox: when there is nothing more to see or do, there is nothing more to look forward to. It's easy to see why surveys of young adults pick up high levels of hopelessness, distrust, cynicism and boredom. Neil Postman wrote a classic book about this very problem called *Amusing Ourselves to Death.*

The unceasing access to pleasure and the consequent unhappiness led evangelist Ravi Zacharias to reference G. K. Chesterton in saying that "meaninglessness ultimately comes not

from being weary of pain but from being weary
of pleasure."[12]

Young adults want to believe that they are
not mere placeholders in history, yet they fear
that what the jaded alter ego Tyler Darden in the
movie "Fight Club" said is true:

> We're the middle children of history . . . no
> purpose or place. We have no Great War, no
> Great Depression. Our great war is a spiritual
> war. Our great depression is our lives.

WHY IT IS SO HARD TO PAY ATTENTION

The young people our organization has
studied spend between 27 and 33 hours per
week using communication technology—gaming,
watching television and movies, text messaging,
instant messaging, and surfing the internet. In
short, they're overwhelmed with information.

Information overload breaks down a person's
capacity for discernment. For example, C. John
Sommerville argued that the 24-hour news cycle
actually makes us dumber, not smarter; it

presents so much information that we find it impossible to figure out what is truly important.[13]

Is it any wonder, then, that only three in ten young adults today embrace the idea of "absolute truth"?[14] Should we be surprised that when asked whether they want to be "a leader in my community" only 12% say yes?[15]

Ask young adults about this lack of civic involvement and you may be surprised by their answers. Just before a recent election, *USA Today* carried an article about why, even with an enormous campaign to encourage them to do so, the vast majority of young adults did not plan to vote. These are actual quotes from the article:

- *Preston, University of North Carolina—* "It's not rational for me to spend my time voting. It's not going to make a difference."
- *Mike, University of Michigan—*"I'm busy. I'm a college student; I don't have the

time. One day I'll do my own research and be knowledgeable enough."

- *Cheryl, New York University*—"I guess I didn't want to go to my elementary school to vote. I don't know, it sounded kind of intimidating—going into a booth and pressing buttons. I don't even know when I can vote. Is it the first week of September?"
- *Albert, New York University*—"I don't care enough to care about why I don't care."
- *Michael, Former voter registration coordinator*—"It's not that I don't care. It's just that I've got more things to worry about, like myself."[16]

The clear sentiment is, "If it's not relevant to *me*, it's not relevant."

THE ANSWER TO THE EVIL

Edmund Burke is famously quoted as saying, "All that is necessary for the triumph of evil is that good men do nothing." What should we call actions that permit evil to triumph? Are they not evil?

The psychic numbing of this generation of young adults is evil precisely because it leads to...nothing. It's not laziness—it's *intentional* noninvolvement: even if they manage to see through the haze of commercialism, young adults have been conditioned to believe that there are no absolute truths, so to "make a difference" would require imposing their will on others, something they refuse to do.

At the outbreak of the Iraq war I was in a hotel room ironing a shirt, watching the television news as a reporter interviewed a series of disaffected college students, asking if they would be willing to fight for their country. One young man summarized the feelings of the group: "Dude, there *is* nothing worth dying for."

Underneath this bravado, however inarticulate, is a barely contained panic. If there is nothing outside of myself by which I can measure my own existence, then I never know where I am. If there is nothing worth *dying* for, then what is worth *living* for?

The question of "What is worth living for?" is why I love being a college professor. A surprising number of my students, having had their fill of meaninglessness, are hungry for spiritual truth.

Sarah Hinlickey explained this in an essay written eight years ago, but which I and my students still find stunningly accurate:

Perhaps the only thing you can do, then, is to point us towards Golgotha, a story that we can make sense of. Show us the women who wept and loved the Lord but couldn't change his fate. Remind us that Peter, the rock of the Church, denied the Messiah three times. Tell us that Pilate washed his hands of the truth, something we are often tempted to do. Mostly, though, turn us towards God hanging on the cross. That is what the world does to the holy. Where the cities of God and Man intersect, there is a crucifixion. The best-laid plans are swept aside; the blueprints for the perfect society are divided among the spoilers. We recognize this world: ripped from the start by our parents' divorces, spoiled by our own bad choices, threatened by war and poverty, pain and meaninglessness. Ours is a world where inconvenient lives are aborted and inconvenient loves are abandoned. We know all too well that we, too, would betray the only one who could save us.[17]

There are only two workable antidotes to information bombardment. The first is to *possess* an authentic narrative that explains the truth in clear terms. The second is to earn the trust needed to *communicate* that narrative in an authentic fashion.

The lack of trust is the sticking point, and as we shall see, it goes both ways. Later in this book you'll learn some powerful ways to develop trust with the next generation. Before we can truly appreciate the cure, however, it is sometimes important to come face to face with the deadly results of the disease.

What the Next Generation is Not Telling You

"The future of civilization depends on our overcoming the meaninglessness and hopelessness that characterizes the thoughts of men today."

Albert Schweitzer

It's easy to understand why so many adults avoid coaching, mentoring or discipling young adults. Just one encounter with a surly teenager—a kid with a hip-hop nonchalance or gruesome multiple body piercings—and you think, "Fine. Be that way. See if I give a rip."

At root, the problem is a lack of trust. You don't trust young adults to act responsibly, and they don't trust you to give advice that is in their best interests.

When I conduct research on youth culture I often ask, "Who do you turn to for advice about the most important issues in life?" About 5% say "coaches," "teachers," or "pastors." About 40% say "parents." The rest, 55%, say "my friends."

Lisa Popyk researched a series of school shootings and found out that the lack of trust between adults and young people can lead to tragedy. Here's some of her report as found in the *Cincinnati Post-Intelligencer*:

On the frigid morning that 16-year-old Evan Ramsey arrived at his Alaska high school carrying a shotgun, a bag of shells and a plan for murder, dozens of students not only knew what was coming, one brought a camera.

When an armed Michael Carneal walked through the doors of his Paducah, Ky., school, one friend bowed his head, closed his eyes and asked God for the strength to make it through the day. He knew, too.

And in Union, Ky., Clay Shrout called an old friend at dawn to describe how he'd just killed his parents and was planning to take hostages at school.

After a 20-minute talk, the friend hung up and headed for school, without a word to anyone. He sat in first period waiting to hear the shots ring out down the hall.

Always, someone knew.

In each of the recent school yard slayings, somebody read the class assignments that ended up being rants on violence and death, someone heard the threats or saw the weapons. Some even helped form the plan. And yet no one spoke up or tried to stop them.

Authorities, parents and teachers are calling it a wall of silence that they are finding frighteningly impenetrable.

Although adolescence always has meant some breakdown in communication with parents and authority figures, rarely have the stakes been so high, said Los Angeles Psychologist Robert R. Butterworth, an expert in youth issues. The children harboring thoughts of violence are like hidden time bombs, Butterworth said.

People are hearing them tick, but they're not telling anyone who or where they are, so authorities can defuse them. If they don't start, he said, the kids are going to keep exploding . . .

In Alaska, authorities believe that 20 to 30 students knew in advance that Evan Ramsey was going to bring a gun to Bethel Regional High School February 19, 1997. Most also knew that the target was Principal Ronald Edwards. But by the time police were finally called, the shooting already had begun.

Principal Edwards was dying in his wife's arms. Not far away, 15-year-old Joshua Palacios was already dead, shot in the stomach as he stood with friends before first bell in the school's common area. The scene still breaks the voice of Sgt. Marrs [the officer called to the scene].

"And in 25 years, I've seen it all," he says. [18]

This is not a failure of institutions. It is a failure of community: a disconnect between generations, a lack of communication, a smoldering resentment, and a popular culture that stokes the fire.

SOMEONE WILL ACT, BUT WHO?

Last year I was gathering information about the history of leadership for my class at Bryan College and came across a few facts about how Constantinople fell to the Muslim invaders in the 1400s. But my question was this: how on earth could the strongest city in the world—spiritually, economically, culturally, and militarily—come to the point of collapse? Through research the pieces fell in place and a chilling picture emerged of parents who chose to let someone else "pass the baton" to their young.

In the 1400s a weakened Christian culture found itself under constant attack by a growing Muslim culture. As Amurath I, ruler of the Ottoman Empire, conquered more and more territory, he decided that if one-fifth of the spoils of battle were the Emperor's share, he should also have a right to one-fifth of the captives.

Amurath instructed his troops to choose the smartest and strongest of the sons of Christian families he had captured. These boys—as young as seven years of age—underwent training in everything from agriculture to statesmanship.

Many Christian parents voluntarily turned their sons over, treating such slavery as a "scholarship" that would guarantee food, supervision, and education to their children. What they didn't seem to realize—or just ignored—was that the young men were being indoctrinated in a fanatical ideology and shaped into a brutal fighting force. They were called the Janizaries.

Over time, the power of the Ottoman Empire grew, while that of eastern Christianity declined. In 1453, hordes of Muslim Ottoman Turks surrounded Constantinople, the seat of the Eastern church. Sultan Mehmet II, a ruthless and shrewd commander just 23 years old, led the siege with 100,000 troops, including 70,000 trained infantry and cavalry, 20,000 skirmishers known for their love of raping and looting, and 10,000 Janizaries.

A mere 7,000 troops rallied to the defense of Constantinople. They were well trained and desperate to protect their families, but weeks of pounding attacks made Mehmet's victory inevitable.

Just as the exhausted defenders steeled themselves for Mehmet's final onslaught, they were frozen by the blood-curdling screams of thousands of young voices: Mehmet had unleashed the elite Janizaries. These young warriors swarmed against the walls, found a breach and charged through, wreaking havoc and slaughter.

The Janizaries had no idea—or didn't care—that their swords were drenched with the blood of their own families.

Someone *will* train the next generation. The question is who, and for what purposes.

It's a massive responsibility with a short time frame. A rapidly growing group of parents, business owners, teachers, coaches, and concerned adults sense—rightly—that no civilization that passed the baton poorly has survived.

Our parents, teachers, coaches, and neighbors passed the baton to us. At least, that's what they should have done. But what if I look back over my life and discover that those who passed the baton to me made a mess of it? What if the people who should have *blessed* me actually *cursed* me?

Those Who Stumbled: Dealing with the Pain of Being Left Out

"Let us now praise famous men, and our fathers that begat us. The Lord hath wrought great glory by them through his great power from the beginning . . . All these were honored in their generations, and were the glory of their times."

Ecclesiasticus 44:1-7

IN GRADE SCHOOL WE PLAYED KICKBALL AT EVERY RECESS. I dreaded this because I knew that when teams were divided I would always be chosen second to last, next to Craig. It wasn't much consolation that I wasn't dead last. Craig was odd and did little to endear himself to others. He smelled funny and had greasy hair and a loud mother and a chaotic home life. I hung out with Craig a little bit, going to his house to watch Three Stooges reruns in his basement. But I didn't want anyone to know he was my friend, even though at various times I didn't have any others competing for that title.

As I think back on it, I realize that most people just avoided Craig, including the teachers, who didn't know what to do with him except give him occasional lectures on personal hygiene. I don't remember his making the transition to junior high with us, or high school. Craig just disappeared.

I picture Craig standing on the track of life saying, "Hey, what about me? Aren't I on the team? When do I get to run my lap?"

I wish that when I was a kid I had had the fortitude to stand up for kids like Craig. There are so many Craigs amongst us—so many who never got a strong baton pass.

Each story is different. Some never got the baton at all. Others had to watch as their parents or caregivers tripped and fell on their faces in front of the whole crowd. Others just got a half-hearted pass. And yet others had the adults in their lives take the baton and use it to beat the stuffing out of them.

We can't go back and change our lives, and yet we are compelled to make sense of events that were often painful. I don't know about you, but I don't feel released to pass the baton to the next generation until I can break the cycle of apathy or cruelty that was passed on to me.

Somehow I've got to figure out how to *honor* those who passed the baton well, and *extend grace* to those who didn't. Sometimes, as in my experience, it's one and the same person.

PA DAN

Pa Dan died on Valentine's Day, ninety years old. At his funeral the children and grandchildren told story after story of his life—evoking side-splitting laughter, singing, and tears.

Pa Dan was my grandpa, and he was a cowboy—not a pretend cowboy, but a real one, from the hills of Oklahoma. He's the guy actor Ben Johnson (the star or co-star of dozens of Western movies) credited with inspiring his career success.

51

In fact, Pa Dan's nickname was "Cowboy"; everybody called him that, including Ben Johnson. Where I grew up in a suburb of Detroit, having a real-life cowboy for a grandpa was a source of inestimable pride.

Yet Pa Dan was a restless soul, and for most of his life he wrestled with God. He drank too much. He and my grandmother argued constantly, and my mother still won't talk about some parts of her growing up years.

Pa Dan never gave me a blessing. He never told me to fulfill my potential. He didn't provide a spiritual example. If I was looking to him for a graceful baton pass, I would be disappointed.

Yet Pa Dan did pass the baton to me, in his own way. He taught me to hunt and fish and play cards and ride a horse. He told stories and stood at the piano to sing cowboy songs; he knew hundreds of them by memory. He took us grandkids along in his pickup and let us drive his Model A Ford.

When I last saw Pa Dan alive, I sensed that in spite of his vigor (he was training a colt and preparing his mare to foal) it would be the last time we saw one another on this earth. We said our goodbyes and I told him I loved him. It was a defining moment for me.

But the defining moment for Pa Dan actually occurred 30 years before my birth. His cowboy-actor-friend Ben Johnson invited him to Hollywood. "Cowboy," he said, "those Hollywood people have more dollars than they have sense, and they're looking for real cowboys. Why don't you come out there with me?"

Cowboy didn't go. Instead, he married Gladys and lived his life in the tiniest of towns, faithful to the Texaco Oil Company. He gave his whole life to that one woman (66 years) and his whole career to that one company (41 years). In the process he influenced four children, 10 grandchildren, and 18 great-grandchildren.

My aunt Pam once asked Ben Johnson, "Was my dad really as great as you said?" Ben replied,

You know, Sis, I owe my entire career to your dad. When we were working cattle in Oklahoma, your dad earned that nickname, "Cowboy". He could out-ride, out-rope, out-shoot all of us and he sure was a darn sight better looking than me. Why, if he had gone to California with me, he would have been the one riding next to John Wayne and I would have just been one of those guys riding behind the sheriff in the posse!

It was an exceedingly gracious thing to say, and it certainly raised Pa Dan's esteem in the eyes of his children.

HONOR AND GRACE

The world did not sit up and take notice when Pa Dan died. Aside from that small crowd of family members and a few friends, no one noticed. It would be easy to conclude that Pa Dan's life didn't mean much.

Seriously, don't the people on TV matter more? Or those in Congress? This is the question asked by virtually every person at one time or another: does my contribution make any difference?

Most people pass into and out of life without much notice. Ashes to ashes, dust to dust. And while they *are* living, life is hard; that's why the biblical word for "labor" is translated "troublesome toil."

Troublesome toil...that's the feeling you get when the alarm clock goes off early even though the kids have been sick all night...when the money just isn't there...when worries press in...when neighbors, friends, co-workers, relatives are just too irritatingly human.

Should I be resentful that Pa Dan gave in to that? Should I be angry that he didn't give me the leg up that my friends' parents and grandparents seemed to give them? Or should I whitewash the past and try to filter out all of the negative things I saw in his life?

The answer to both questions is no. Let's find out why.

Finding—and Sharing—the Meaning in Your Life Experiences

"The purpose of life is a life of purpose."
Robert Byrne

Both the Inner Giver and the Inner Taker are present in everyone. I can express honor for the times when those who went before me became givers. But I also extend grace for the times when they were takers. Honor and grace are two sides of the same coin. I rejoice in the times when they generously picked me up by my bootstraps, and I mourn the times when I got bruised in the collision with their injured souls.

Honor and grace always—always—go hand in hand.

Pa Dan was far from perfect. In fact, in many ways, he was a scoundrel. Yet I can honor Pa Dan for the virtue of humility. He never pretended to be someone he wasn't. He never faked belief in something he didn't really believe. He lived a life full of choices, some good, some bad, and passed the baton to a generation of children and grandchildren who graduated from college and became managers, teachers, musicians, investment advisors and professors.

And I can also show grace to Pa Dan in the same way that he showed grace to me. He never brought up what it cost to fix Uncle Dewayne's pickup truck window after my brother Scott and I shot it out. He never mocked my fear of horses. He didn't speak derisively of me when I wanted to get a Ph.D., even though his upbringing might have caused him to despise anything so "high brow."

I have been the recipient of grace and I can extend grace to Pa Dan. I can mourn the fact that those who passed the baton to him passed it poorly, and I can marvel at how well he did in spite of that handicap.

This only goes so far, of course. It's easy to extend grace to one who was sometimes grumpy and distant. It's another matter entirely to do so for someone who was abusive and cruel. Where is the meaning in that?

Sometimes the answers don't come. As the singer/songwriter Michael Card once noted in a talk at our leadership camp, "Most people go to the grave with their most pressing questions unanswered."

That's why the virtue of humility that I learned from Pa Dan is so important. It's painful to admit that I don't have all the answers, and that I can't make my life turn out the way I want.

Everyone to whom I owe debts of gratitude was deeply flawed. The first step in my preparing to pass the baton is to express honor and grace to *them*. Here are some of those to whom I am indebted:

- R. could be distant and uncommunicative, but he taught me to have integrity.
- S. once cruelly punished me in front of my classmates, but he also refused to let me give in to physical weakness.

- B. had some weird political views, but she taught me the value of persistence.

When I start thinking this way, thankfulness flows:

- D. was a passive mentor who gave little direction, but taught me to be a lifelong learner.
- S. was a self-centered materialist who boldly confronted my feelings of self-pity.
- N. struggled with depression, but ignited my love for history.
- I learned the pain of alcohol abuse from the sad life of O., who was a generous and kind friend.
- D. never answered my hard questions about God, but I never forgot his simple faith.

Make your list. What did you learn about how to treat people? What did you learn about how *not* to treat people? Whatever your experience, pass it on.

MAKING SENSE OF IT ALL

It's not that hard to pass on your life lessons, really. Invite a young person for coffee, and say, "I've learned a lot in my years and I'd like to pass some of the lessons on to a worthy person. Maybe I could help you find a sense of direction in life."

Ask thought-provoking questions:

- Why do you think you were born at this moment in history?
- Why do you suppose God gave you the family he did?
- What sorts of things have you accomplished which gave you a tremendous sense of satisfaction?
- What would you share with others if you only had one thing left to say?
- Time and money aside, what would you rather be doing?

While you're asking questions, do some baton passing:

- Say how meaningful his contribution is, and to whom.
- Give an idea of the important role he plays.
- Parents and grandparents: Show baby pictures and tell the story of his birth.
- Impart a sense of history—what has happened to your company, family, church, or neighborhood over time.
- Let him see you "in action" making a difference for others.
- Convey your unconditional love, *and* your undying commitment to help him live a meaningful life.

Those who influenced me were recipients of honor and grace, and so am I. Yet I am not justified in being passive toward the next generation in the hope that they'll honor me and extend grace to those around them. I can't just eat my bread and let them take whatever crumbs fall.

There is a better way, as I learned from Peep the duck.

Planting Seeds of Blessing

"May God in Heaven fulfill abundantly the prayers which are pronounced over you and your boats and equipment on the occasion of the Blessing of the Fleet. God bless your going out and coming in; The Lord be with you at home and on the water. May he accompany you when you start on your many journeys; May he fill your nets abundantly as a reward for your labor; And may he bring you all safely in, when you turn your boats homeward to shore. Amen."

Blessing of the Fleet
Bayou La Batre, Alabama

YEARS AGO A BEST-SELLING BOOK SPOKE OF HOW IMPORTANT IT IS FOR CHILDREN to have a blessing from their parents. I never did read the book, but just knowing the idea made me want to pass a baton of blessing to the next generation.

The word "blessing" comes from two Greek words, *eu* (well) and *logos* (word): to speak well of. That's where we get our word "eulogy." The most common place for a eulogy is at a funeral, to speak well of a person's life once he is gone.

But what if we didn't wait until people were gone? What if we could work up the nerve to tell them what their gifts and character mean to us and others while they are yet alive? What difference would that make?

Peep, We Hardly Knew Ye

I have attended a lot of funerals and have been "on the program" in a few. Yet, oddly, what it means to eulogize became most clear as I walked with my then six-year-old son Graham through the funeral of Peep the duck.

I didn't grow up on a farm and know very little about animals, a fact I've found embarrassing all of my life. My most vivid memory of a farm was the day I spent as a small child with one of my mother's childhood friends, Judy, and her large-handed husband whose name I have forgotten.

The man took me out into a pasture in his pickup so we could rescue a sick calf. He picked it up with his large hands and brought it to the truck, whereupon he opened the passenger door and dropped the poor bawling thing at my feet. I had no idea that calves could be so scary.

Then we went back to the barn to milk a cow. All I had to do was bring a bucket of milk to Miss Judy, but I tripped and fell in a puddle and spilled the milk all over myself.

I know you're not supposed to cry over that, but I did. Miss Judy's large-handed husband lifted me up as gently as he could, in a gruff sort of way, and brought me back to the house where Miss Judy stripped off my clothes and threw them in the wash and I watched television in my underwear, wrapped in an afghan.

Miss Judy and my mother had a good laugh about that, but my father's expression was more pained. He hadn't been raised on a farm either, and I think he felt sorry for me.

So when I grew up and got married and had a son, I wanted life to be different. We moved to the country and fixed up an old house. We started with animals gradually. First was a cat, Danger, and the neighbor's dog, Buddy, who moved into our breezeway, but things accelerated from there and before long we were raising chickens.

On my list of things to want, it never occurred to me to write "chickens." But Danielle had grown up on a farm with lots of animals and was very comfortable with domesticated birds. In fact, her father races pigeons, which is one of the more unusual sports in America. I think wild birds are okay, but domestic birds, whether in the cage or in the yard, are fussy and noisy, and they look at you funny with one eye.

When Danielle's father came to visit us, he set about fixing up an old shed to be a chicken coop. He worked so hard that I felt guilty and agreed to get chickens.

I had no idea what I was in for. By the end of the project, when raccoons came and ate them all during Christmas vacation, I had fed, watered, and played with the chickens, repaired the coop, trapped invading carnivores including a skunk (which is a whole other story), and even felt a twinge of sadness when one or another of the chickens' lives ended prematurely.

Still nothing about this period of my life forms a more poignant memory than what happened to Peep, the duck that sort of "came along" with the chickens.

Where we live people bring their animals to town to sell. Puppies, kittens, chicks, and ducks are available on any given Saturday at the Tractor Supply. While Danielle gathered supplies for the chickens, Graham happened to spy a little lame duckling, all lonely in the duck box after its sisters and brothers had been snapped up by the customers.

Graham's long gazes and tender caresses were noticed by the duck vendor, who gave the little duckling to my son as a gift. Graham named it Peep. I was not there that day, but when I got home and saw Peep and heard the story, I wondered what kind of uncertain grace it was for the duck vendor to give a lame duckling to a little boy. A lame duck, as you know from

the use of the term in politics, can't do anything.
It will die and there is nothing you can do about
it.

My son did not know this, and for two days
Graham loved Peep with all his heart. Peep's
poor state only deepened his compassion. We
played with Peep on the kitchen table and talked
lovingly to him and even made a little box for
him next to Graham's bed.

On the morning of the second day, however,
we awoke to find Peep's little body still and cold.
I have never seen such a sad little boy, and it
occurred to me that it was my responsibility, as a
papa, to handle the burial and funeral. Graham
and I put on our shoes and I got the shovel and
we walked, arm in arm, to the edge of the woods.

One spade full of dirt made a big enough
hole, and Graham gently laid Peep in the
ground. I scooped the dirt back over with my
hands and placed a marker on top, because
Graham was worried that I would run over
Peep's body with the lawn tractor.

Graham cried and I felt awful, because I knew that Peep's death was inevitable but could not ease my son's feeling of loss.

Having only known Peep for a day, I didn't really have anything to say at our funeral service. So I asked Graham, "Do you want to say anything?"

"Peep was a good little duck," Graham began, and waxed eloquent for several minutes, his words occasionally interrupted by sobs. An amazing depth of attachment had developed in less than 48 hours between my son and that little duckling.

I thought of a few things to say about how much joy Peep had brought us during his short life, and then we walked slowly back to the house.

In reflecting on that event, what struck me about Graham's little-kid eulogy for Peep was that he didn't talk at all about what he had done for Peep—"Peep, I fed you and watered you and made a box with a soft washcloth to sleep on"—

but what Peep had done for him, such as (this is my grown-up spin on it, of course) awakened his sense of paternal responsibility, delighted his spirit with its innocence, and stirred his compassion for the weak and helpless.

And Peep had done all this in less than two days. This made me suspect that heartache somehow fits into God's plan, because the seemingly meaningless tragedy of Peep's birth defect, and his premature death, once we had acknowledged what it had done for us, deepened my young son's soul, and mine too.

WHAT A BLESSING DOES

A blessing, a eulogy, doesn't start out as a charge, but as an acknowledgement, "Here is what I see in you that makes a great deal of difference to me." I don't know what it is about human beings, but we need that. We crave it. Whenever the Spirit leads me to bless others, I watch as they grow quiet and their ears open up big. Their eyes say, "Woo-HOO!"

I'm the same way. When someone speaks a word of blessing to me, it's like a sincere hug to the soul. Those simple words, even if the person doesn't know me well, acknowledge what a difference my life has made and prophesy about what a difference it could make in the future. Such words tug the padlock off of the closet where I keep the kind of hopes and dreams that begin with, "I could do this, except . . ."

To *receive* a blessing is to be released from the insincere expectations of society. To *give* a blessing is to set others free. We all have the master key. I wonder what would happen if we made it part of the life ritual, rather than the death ritual. I sometimes think that if I did nothing more than pass a baton of blessing to the next generation it would be enough.

But what does it mean to *really* bless someone beyond merely speaking some kind words to them? I picked up the answer one day watching a friend teach his little girl to ride a bicycle.

Riding the Bicycle: Six Steps to Building Trust with the Next Generation

"Tell me and I'll forget; show me and I may remember; involve me and I'll understand."

Chinese Proverb

Two summers ago during the slow moments of a conference on our campus, I passed the time watching one of our coaches teach his daughter to ride a bike. He gently guided her, encouraged her, walked alongside her, released her, and stood guard over her when she quavered. It occurred to me that passing the baton of blessing is like that. It's not some complex function requiring U.N. officials and government pronouncements. In fact, it's very simple:

1. See their souls. As that daddy marched down the sidewalk by his daughter's side all I saw was an absurdly large helmet and pads everywhere. But that daddy saw the little girl's soul. He knew something of her strengths, weaknesses, gifts, fears, and joys. He knew that it would have been easier to *not* teach her to ride because the transition to bicycle freedom can be painful. That daddy loved his daughter just the way she was, but he also loved her too much to leave her that way.

Passing the baton of blessing is like that: love people enough to move them beyond where they are. King Solomon was thought by the ancient Israelites to be the wisest man who ever lived. Among his many sayings was this nugget: "Train a child in the way he should go; even when he is old he will not depart from it." The phrase "in the way he should go" literally means "according to his *bent*." To successfully train a child, I work with what the good Lord put there, bringing out *his* best, not merely reproducing *my* best in *him*.

2. Show the way. As I watched that daddy patiently guide his daughter toward bicycle freedom, I could see him pointing to their destination. "We're going to go down to there and turn around." She needed him to do that—to help her set a goal.

To pass a baton of blessing to the next generation, I must cast a vision: "*Here* is where we are; *there* is where we ought to be." Another of Solomon's wise sayings: "Where there is no prophetic vision the people cast off restraint." Andy Stanley calls it "visioneering." That's helpful—someone's got to keep us from running in circles. More often than not it happens in little snippets of conversation:

- "This is what's important in life."
- "For much of my life I lived like _____. Now I see there is a better way."
- "If you don't do anything else in life, do this."
- "Whatever else happens, don't forget _____."

3. Strengthen the spirit. As that daddy guided his daughter down the sidewalk, I could see the fear in her face. He must have known she was afraid, because he kept leaning down to whisper to her. I imagine what he was whispering: "You can do this!" "I am holding on to you!" "Keep going!" "Good job!"

A blessing means encouragement. To *en*courage means "to give courage to." The wise mentor raises the bar. My kids, my students, don't need me to say, "You're just fine the way you are." They need me to say, "It's hard, but I know you can do this."

4. Step alongside. That little girl might never have learned to ride a bike if her daddy hadn't stepped alongside to guide her. It's true for all of us in every area of life. Every Odysseus needs a Mentor. Every Elisha needs an Elijah. Every Frodo Baggins needs a Gandalf. It's one thing to say, "Get out there and do it." It's another thing to step alongside.

Because of a speaking invitation, Danielle and I got to go to Hawaii a couple of years ago. Each person we met asked, "Is this your first time in Hawaii?" When we said yes, they replied cheerfully, "Well, *aloha*!" "Aloha," we discovered, means so much more than "hello."

"Alo" means presence and "ha" means breath. Literally, aloha means the presence of divine breath. To say "aloha" is to quite literally ask, "How may I be the presence of the divine to you?" or, "How may I breathe the divine into you?" It's a wonderful prayer, rooted in the creation story of God breathing life into man, and an awesome representation of what I must do for the next generation—breathe life into them. Help them be filled with life so that they might truly live, and in turn, breathe life into others.

It's not just a one-time thing like blowing up a beach ball. It's walking beside, showing, encouraging, pleading, blessing, coaxing, reminding, encouraging again, correcting, back-slapping, scolding, hugging, and encouraging again.

5. Send ahead. When I trained my son Graham to ride a bike, I knew there would be a point at which I would have to let go. I felt horrible because I *knew* that he would wobble into the ditch and get hurt. But to my amazement, he straightened up and kept going. Only then did I realize that my holding *on* was actually holding him *back*: to ride, he needed to go faster than I could run.

To send the next generation ahead, I've got to equip them with the skills they need to win, help them clearly see who they are and what they can accomplish, and then choose the right time and place to make the transition.

6. Stand guard. A child learning to ride a bike is destined to crash. It's better for us parents if we acknowledge that up front. It's not that we *hope* they crash, but that we know—and they don't—that crashing is part of learning to ride.

A distressed parent called me one day, upset over a teenage daughter who had gone astray. "What should I do? All of my hopes have been dashed," she said.

I don't know if what I told her was good advice or not, but here it is: "Imagine in your mind the most sinful action your daughter could take. Decide that even if she did *that*, you'll love her anyway, and *fight* for her restoration."

Over the last 20 years of leadership training, I've had the opportunity to work with thousands of young people. When one succeeds, I'm thrilled. But many fail, and it's heartbreaking. A lot of mentoring is repair work—coming alongside those who have given up, tattered and ashamed, gently pulling them to their feet, brushing them off, and strengthening their spirits once more.

That's how to give a blessing: see the soul, show the way, strengthen the spirit, step alongside, send ahead, and stand guard. It's that simple, and it's that complex. What remains is to practice each of these until they become reflexive.

Of course, they will inevitably be curious about your own life experiences. "Did you learn to ride?" "What was it like?" As with every other thing, your life teaches. What will it say?

Lessons from a Sled Dog: What You Cannot *Not* Do

"Don't worry that children never listen to you; worry that they are always watching you."

Robert Fulghum

ON JUNE 12, 2004, I BECAME A CLICHÉ, at least according to the *Des Moines Register*. The reporter covering my graduation speech to the state's homeschool graduates wrote: "Keynote speaker Jeffrey Myers urged students to look inward for the key to a happy and fulfilling future."

That wasn't really my point, but I can't blame the author for reporting it that way. After all, doesn't every graduation speaker offer some version on that theme?

"Follow your dreams," we say. Impatient grads roll their eyes: "As if I wouldn't!" But adults in the audience react differently. They recall *their* graduation—ten years ago, twenty years ago, maybe more—and unconsciously review the lives they've lived since.

When I graduated from high school my classmates and I were full of hope. Even at our five-year reunion, we still had that "conquer the world" attitude—introducing fiancées and handing out freshly minted business cards as the sound system pumped out Timbuk 3's hit "My Future's So Bright I Gotta Wear Shades."

But something happened by the ten-year reunion. People got married to their less-than-ideal partner. They divorced. They mastered their job and were bored to tears, or they bumped up against the glass ceiling and were dissatisfied.

Substance abuse. Heartache. Emptiness. Despair. I was surprised at how many of my classmates were so afflicted. We had all the advantages—no one went off to war, and the economy was bustling. The rampant cynicism my classmates displayed told the truth, not about the world, but about us. Very few of us were fabulously rich, but by the world's standards, we were all wealthy. We found, though, that the material success we longed for, and that our teachers and parents longed for us to have, was a false friend.

Now when I speak at graduations, I scan the audience wondering how many listen to the hopefulness with a dark secret, the whisper of the heart: "For me, life didn't work that way."

Is There More?

My classmates and I believed that material success would redeem us. Most found it, in varying degrees. Business owners, investors, sales professionals, doctors, lawyers, and one or two professors—we succeeded far beyond what our parents' generation had ever hoped for. But we also began to sense that working for a paycheck, in and of itself, is meaningless—even if it is a *good* paycheck. So we began asking, "Is there more?"

I'd like to think there is more. I'd love to wake up each day and live my dreams. But it's tough to figure out exactly how I would do this. I don't even have the vocabulary for it. I was trained to talk about "jobs" and "careers" as if the path to survival and success was "out there" somewhere.

But what if success was more about finding your *calling* than getting a *job*? What if the important thing were not making a living, but making a life? What if, instead of beguiling others into thinking we're something we're not, we sought to become everything we were designed to be? Would there be joy in that?

In a perfect world your calling would produce immense satisfaction. But the world we inhabit doesn't operate like that. It's as if you have in mind a glorious painting, but the more you paint, the more your despair grows—the brushes aren't cooperating and the colors seem a little dull and the proportions are all wrong. The reality falls short of what you know to be the painting's genuine potential.

Is it really possible to paint this glorious painting with our gifts? There is a secret that I learned about seven years ago, from a dog, which makes me think the answer is yes.

I Wanna Be a Sled Dog

"Jeff, our group would like to invite you to come to Alaska to speak. We'll pay your honorarium, airfare, hotel and meals. We'd like to pay your wife's expenses so she can come with you, and we'll spring for a three-day tour around our great state."

That's how I knew it was the Lord's will to go to Alaska.

Danielle and I arrived in Anchorage during the running of the Iditarod, the legendary sled dog race covering more than 1,000 miles of Alaska wilderness—mountains, plains, forests, even frozen lakes and rivers.

The Iditarod is perhaps the most strenuous test of human (or animal) endurance anywhere in the world. Racers and their teams are all alone—often in complete darkness—carrying all the supplies they'll need along the way. For more than 1,000 miles.

I watched the dogs. I toured race headquarters. I reveled in the history of the great event—it's a memorial to a 1925 relay made famous by the lead dog, Balto, guiding Gunnar Kaasen through winds of 80 miles per hour to deliver life-saving serum to Nome, ravaged by diphtheria.

There was only one thing left to do: find someone who would give me the *experience* of being a musher. Fortunately, a local hobbyist agreed to treat Danielle and me to a dog sled adventure. We arrived at his home and saw the 25 sled dogs, each of which *begged* piteously to be taken along—barking, growling, lunging, foaming at the mouth. It seemed as if each dog was saying, "Ooh, ooh, ooh! Pick me! Pick me!"

Our host, William, chose eight and began harnessing them to the sled. The remaining 17 dogs were in various stages of nervous breakdown at the thought of being left behind. One, sensing that she was one of the non-elect, moaned, groaned, strained against her leash, lunged and flipped over. Again and again she tried in vain to get William's attention.

Awed by her determination, I said, "William, I think that dog would like to go with us."

William glanced over his shoulder and mumbled, "She can't go. She's injured."

Observing her painful antics, I could easily see how she might injure herself. As we headed off down the trail, she broke free and ran after us, dragging the chain and anchor behind her. "I'm *so sorry* I'm late! I got held up a little bit!" she seemed to say. William gave in, attached her to the harness and off we went.

It was a beautiful, sunny, clear day for drinking in the sights and sounds of the stunning Alaskan wilderness. "A little too warm for the dogs," William remarked matter-of-factly at the 20-degree Fahrenheit reading. Each time we stopped, the dogs collapsed, panting, and buried their noses in the snow. It was obviously hard work pulling the sled, but they didn't even mind.

William managed the chaos of the now nine energetic dogs with a quiet calm. If he wanted them to go right, he'd whisper, "Gee." If he wanted them to go left, he'd whisper, "Haw." Instant obedience.

Returning to base, I blurted, "William, we have a dog that lives at our house, and he only obeys when we yell at him. Yet you get obedience through a whisper. What's up?"

"Jeff," William said, "Those dogs were made for this. They live for this. And when you're doing what God designed you to do, your master can guide you with a whisper."

William's reply stunned me. In fact, it opened up a whole new way to live joyfully. Give me a few moments and I'll explain how.

Living to Be, Not to Have

"If you want to feel rich, just count the things you have
that money can't buy"

Unknown

It was not until the return flight home from Alaska that the majesty of William's remark began to sink in. He was using the example of the sled dogs to explain how God guides us most clearly when we're operating in our gifts.

Those animals taught me that I want to be a "sled dog" about the most important things in life. I want to live with joy—even when life is tough.

Psalm 139:13-14 (ESV) says, "For you formed my inward parts; you knitted me together in my mother's womb. I praise you, for I am fearfully and wonderfully made. Wonderful are your works; my soul knows it very well."

If I'm designed to be a sled dog, though, why do I see a junkyard hound in the mirror? With whose eyes am I looking at myself?

Maybe I'm shallow, but I think I see myself mainly through the eyes of the companies that want to sell me things. They're ruthless and persistent: "You fall short, and everyone seems to know it but you. Never fear, though, we can restore you to adequacy. Just buy 'X.'"

Grills are even sold this way—if you buy the right grill girls in bikinis will come to your house to eat. If you don't, well, it's a free country, but don't hold us responsible if you stay lonely.

The culture of advertising thrives by spawning dissatisfaction. Actors look a lot sexier putting on their deodorant than I do. Maybe if I buy those products a little of their coolness will rub off on me.

Our local 24/7 Stuff Mart put in televisions last year to remind shoppers of the things they forgot they needed. For several months they ran a commercial with a country music crooner singing, "You Can't Out-Love Your Underwear." They played this advertisement, literally, every five minutes. The particular clothing company sponsoring this commercial had a website where you could download this self-proclaimed "smash hit."

It's catchy, I'll admit. I annoyed myself humming the tune. Sometimes I wished I could hit the reset button on my brain and forget I ever knew stuff like that.

If the advertisements themselves don't drive you to despair, the fact that you can't have everything you want *will.* If my life is what I possess, and I don't possess much, then what is my life worth? The universe that was my friend becomes my tormentor.

A friend of mine tells the story of visiting a museum exhibit containing the personal effects of a long-dead Russian Czar, including the Czar's toothbrush. My friend stared at it for a few minutes and had an epiphany: the Czar has been dead for 100 years, but his *toothbrush* was still here? He was out-lasted by his *toothbrush*?

Life is too short to be obsessed with things that will take up space in landfills long after we're gone. But it's hard for young adults today to see this; having been raised to consume rather than produce, they still think they can buy their way to happiness. Sadly, many adults believe this as well, and it taints the advice we give to the next generation.

"It costs a lot to keep up," we say, "so you'd better get a good-paying job." We tell the dreamers, "It's nice that you want to be an artist, but why don't you go ahead and get that engineering degree so that [everyone together now . . .] *you have something to fall back on?*"

I hear this from kids all the time. "I want to teach in the inner city, but my dad says I need to go to nursing school because nurses can make more money." "I want to be a missionary, but my mom says she wants me to be close by so she can see the grandkids more easily." "I'd really like to build things, but my teacher says that the serious money is in computers."

I'll admit that in these situations parents might be discerning character flaws that I can't see. But let's be honest. How much of our planning and strategizing actually has the effect of reproducing our mistakes in the next generation? Is this not unconsciously passing the baton of fear to the next generation?

Much of what passes for concern these days is utilitarianism, pure and simple. Perhaps *capitulation* is a better word. "I fell into the trap and it's painful, so you'd better get ready so that when you fall into the trap it doesn't hurt as much."

We need a whole new way of conversing with the next generation about what is important. Here are some starters:

- "Let's figure out a way to do this that works *with* your design instead of *against* it."
- "When I was your age I went for the secure job even though I didn't like it. There were benefits, sure, but there were costs, too."
- "Why don't we try a bunch of things and see what really lights your fire?"

- "Let's not just figure out what you can do. Let's figure out what you cannot *not* do."
- "Everybody works differently. Let's see if we can look back over your life to see *how* you work and *why* you do what you do."
- "I'm committed to helping you figure out how to thrive by doing what you really are designed to do."

These are the conversations that the younger generation is yearning to have. And they assume that you have the answer because, well, you're older. Even if you're just a few years ahead they assume that you've had a chance to explore the paths of failure enough to put up warning signs.

Everybody needs someone to turn around, look at them, and say, "Keep going. There's something out there you can be a sled dog for. I'm looking for it, too. Let's walk together."

There's a problem, though. What if they won't listen?

How to Get the Attention of the Next Generation (Without Yelling)

"In everyone's life, at some time, our inner fire goes out. It is then burst into flame by an encounter with another human being. We should all be thankful for those people who rekindle the inner spirit."

Albert Schweitzer

I CAN'T EVEN IMAGINE IT HAPPENING IN A RELAY but I suppose it's possible: a runner finishes his lap and the next runner refuses to take the baton pass. It's really an absurd picture, but in the race of life it happens all the time.

Look back over your own life. Even if someone had tried to pass the baton to you, there's a pretty good chance that at many points in your life you would have refused it.

Every generation thinks it knows better than the previous one. They look at their technological prowess and cultural awareness and assume, mistakenly, that their values are also better. They never come right out and say it, of course, but you can see it in their eyes: "I appreciate your effort, you elderly person, but I know better."

That stings, but it's pretty good payback for the generation whose motto was, "Never trust anyone over 30," don't you think?

But seriously, how *do* you get the younger generation to take the baton? If every generation has faced this problem, surely someone has come up with a solution. Fortunately someone has. Solomon, the wisest man who ever lived, wrote an entire book, Proverbs, about it. His strategy? Beg. Solomon begged his son to pursue wisdom and flee foolishness. Apparently, pleading is a fine art mastered only by the wisest people. You can hear Solomon's petitions in almost every chapter:

- Proverbs 1:8 (ESV)—Hear, my son, your father's instruction..."
- Proverbs 3:1 (ESV)—My son, do not forget my teaching, but let your heart keep my commandments..."

- Proverbs 4:10 (ESV)—Hear my son, and accept my words, that the years of your life may be many.
- Proverbs 4:20 (ESV)—My son, be attentive to my words; incline your ear to my sayings."
- Proverbs 5:1 (ESV)—My son, be attentive to my wisdom; incline your ear to my understanding..."
- Proverbs 7:1 (ESV)—My son, keep my words and treasure up my commandments with you..."

Begging is not weakness; it takes tremendous strength to call another person out of foolishness into wisdom. Without someone to call them out, a generation cannot grow wise. Unless you and I intervene, foolishness is the likely outcome in this generation. Or any generation for that matter.

Indeed, in today's pop culture, foolishness is the only likely outcome, short of intervention. Americans see, on average, 28 hours of television a week. (One of my students said,

"Twenty-eight hours? Man, they're missing a lot of great shows." He was joking. I think.) These viewers absorb an average of one act of sexual intercourse and two murders per hour, and are filling their minds with sexual innuendo and gratuitous violence as harmless humor.

In Proverbs Solomon points out that there is a way that leads to life and a way that leads to death. Few people choose the path of death intentionally. Rather, they start out on that path thinking that it will bring them life, and by the time they discover their error, they believe that it is too late to reverse course.

Left to themselves, the vast majority of people just ease on down the road, making decisions based on what will bring amusement ("amuse" literally means "to not think").

How do you call someone out of foolishness without seeming weak or pathetic? Consider these conversation openers:

- "Please listen very carefully for a moment. I have something I'd like to tell you that could have a big influence on your life."
- "Could you meet my eyes for a moment? There's something very important I want to tell you."
- "So much depends on what I'm about to share with you. Please give me your full attention."

I would be unlikely to pass the baton to someone who doesn't want it except for my encounter with a person who did it to me, or should I say *for* me?

HEY, YOU, LISTEN

"This could be the best year of your life or the worst year of your life, depending on whether you listen to me."

That's the first thing Dr. Mary Rowland ever said to me. As you might expect, I found her maternal bossiness unnerving. Dr. Rowland was Vice President for Student Life, the one charged with checking the abuses of power cooked up by the little tyrants who got elected to student government.

That included me. I was the newly elected student government president, ready to reclaim the Sixties and give the university administration ulcers. My friends even said to me, "Don't listen to Dr. Rowland—she's just trying to control you."

The fact is, however, I had no idea what I was doing. With a one-vote margin of victory (always vote for yourself, by the way), my hold on power was tenuous, and warring factions of student groups were eager to do battle. I knew where I wanted to go, and had a budget of several hundred thousand dollars to work with, but I had no idea how to get there.

Dr. Rowland started by helping me rehabilitate our disgustingly shabby student government offices. It was her idea, for example, to take all of our old desks and filing cabinets down to the auto-body paint shop to be spray-painted coordinating colors.

The effect was immediate. The refurbished office instantly raised my credibility. Obviously, when that happened, my opinion of Dr. Rowland changed. She had tilted things in my favor through a simple act that was almost an afterthought for her. Was I now willing to listen? You'd better believe it. (Lesson: prove that what you're saying works—don't just expect others to take your word for it.)

When Dr. Rowland insisted on having a strategic planning retreat with the student senate, however, I thought she'd finally gotten in over her head. "Dr. Rowland," I said, "I *promise* you that you don't want all those people together in the same room for a whole day."

"Nonsense," she replied. "We'll have it at my house—there are so many valuable antiques they won't dare move a muscle." She was right. I've never seen so many people with rowdy reputations on such good behavior.

Dr. Rowland showed me how to become credible in the eyes of my classmates. She instructed me in the political fineries of making peace between the Alpha Delta and Phi Delta Theta fraternities, the African American group and the Viet Nam Veterans group, the communications department and the student newspaper, and in several other petty turf wars.

As a result, our student government experienced unprecedented unity. We accomplished valuable projects that still benefit Washburn University students to this day.

All told, Dr. Rowland invested about thirty hours in my life during that year, time that dramatically advanced my own leadership ability, transformed our student government, and equipped me to coach two successive student government presidents.

WALKING WITH THEM

Dr. Rowland *lived* leadership in front of me until I became the leader I was meant to be. She helped me gain favor with those I led and strengthened me into a good leader. I don't think a day goes by when I don't apply some lesson I learned from Dr. Rowland all those years ago.

As I approached graduation, Dr. Rowland wrote glowing letters of recommendation for graduate school. She sent a card on my birthday. When I was sidelined by a serious car accident, she was the first to call. We became friends, as much as a rail-thin College Republican fraternity kid and a rail-thin liberal 48-year-old chain-smoking Methodist laywoman could be.

About a year after my graduation I received shocking news. Dr. Rowland was dead of a brain aneurysm.

I asked to write the tribute in our alumni magazine in which I said, in essence, "Mary Rowland led as Jesus led." I didn't have any vague, mushy sentiment in mind when I said that—I meant it quite literally. Gűnter Krallmann in his book *Mentoring for Missions*, writes:

Through the disciples' continual exposure to who he was, what he did and said, Jesus... desired them to become so saturated with the influences arising from his example and teaching, his attitudes, actions, and anointing, that every single area of their lives would be impacted toward greater likeness to himself.[19]

Everyone knows that the greatest lessons in life are *caught,* not *taught.* But what this really means is that if you want to influence people, you have to walk with them until some of *you* rubs off onto *them.* As we shall see, this means doing at least three things differently.

Three Ways to Have a Lasting Impact on Others, Starting Today

"Remember, man does not live on bread alone: sometimes he needs a little buttering up."
John Maxwell

In college I interned for an advertising agency and was assigned to the department that buys advertising time on television and radio stations. My supervisor didn't have the foggiest idea how to mentor, but her instincts were right. She said, "Put your desk outside my office door and listen to everything that happens." As I completed my work, I overheard her conversations and learned what to do—and what *not* to do.

To really disciple others means allowing them to absorb your mannerisms, your habits and how you handle situations. Your reflexes become their reflexes. Jesus was so close to his disciples that they even began to *act* like him. Everyone could tell they had been with Jesus.

Few of us have hours and hours to spend with those we're influencing. Yet if we can do the three following things differently, the time we *do* invest will yield greater returns:

1. Impart Meaning Through Specificity

If you tell someone "good job," it makes him smile. But if you give a specific description of what you noticed, his eyes lock on to you with great intensity and he really *listens*.

Specificity is a blessing: like a musician tuning a string to perfect pitch, you can concentrate a person on living out his gifts gloriously.

I became convinced at an early age that career tests or personality and social styles analyses are not the best way to do this. My high school career test revealed that I could be a lumberjack. This was ironic in that I was the skinniest kid in my school and had never held a chain saw. After all, at 6'1" and 140 pounds (I was 140 because I had beefed up during my senior year), I wasn't even sure I *could* hold a chainsaw.

Such tests can be helpful, but they are limited because they evaluate you by comparing you to others, and you *aren't* anyone else. You're *you.* Your goal in life is not to become what other people are, but to become everything God designed you to be.

A friend of mine, Wayne, invested most of his career on a military base doing accounting, processing travel vouchers, and generating payroll. Wayne was a good father, a faithful husband, an active church member. But he didn't relish his work.

After his retirement, I asked Wayne, "What did you do to make your work meaningful?" He replied, "I prayed specifically for every person whose check I was writing or whose travel voucher I was processing." From this and other comments, Wayne's gifting suddenly emerged with sparkling clarity: he was Barnabas to the Apostle Paul, an encourager.

Rather than being driven to despair by his job, Wayne's persistence in giving meaning to his work positioned him to live out his true gifts. His lack of meaning at work, ironically, gave him a greater sensitivity to how others could live their gifts.

Because of his gifting, Wayne even spent the first two years of his retirement working in our organization as our CEO: "Chief Encouragement Officer." He loved, encouraged, and equipped our clients as they sought to train the next generation of leaders. He became the most natural baton passer I know.

2. PRACTICE ACCEPTANCE

Some in the younger generation fear that they won't meet the standards of the older generation. That's why they don't talk to you— they think you'll be disappointed. Others don't think they need you. They've become accustomed to living the way they want, and your influence is an intrusion.

Most people just back off. Those who are too stubborn to do that take a hard line: "I don't care if you like it, you *will* do it my way." This is fine if you know that what you require is based on standards that are timeless and true.

But be careful, in calling someone to change for the better, you don't attack his identity. Most people could identify a Mercedes Benz automobile if they saw one on the road. There are certain lines, certain identifying features that distinguish a Mercedes Benz from other vehicles. It's possible to identify a Mercedes Benz whether it came off of the assembly line 50 years ago or yesterday. Mercedes Benz designers are careful to improve their vehicles without changing that fundamental identity.

In a similar way, each person has a shape that we must affirm, not change. It's infinitely more complex to work with a shape of a person than to start from scratch. But with people, starting from scratch is not an option. Their identities, their life experiences, have already shaped them. We affirm what is there and work to bring out its true glory.

Some fear that accepting people just the way they are will take away their motivation to excel. Actually, the opposite is true, as Bill Thrall and his co-authors emphasize in *The Ascent of a Leader*:

> If people affirm us for who we are, this ignites a desire to please them. If we love and are loved in spite of what we know about others or what they know about us, we become empowered to change for the better. . . . Practicing acceptance does not mean we abandon performance standards or accountability in our organizations. . . . An organization without accountability is a ship without a rudder. But to maintain a basis for healthy accountability, the organization must also accept its role as a community.[20]

By both accepting and challenging the next generation, you gain the credibility to motivate them to great deeds.

3. BLESS AND DO NOT CURSE

Interviews and study of child development convince me that somewhere between the ages of nine and eleven children decide to either become "influencers" or the "influenced." The influencers are more likely to lead, and the influenced are likely to succumb to peer pressure. The expectations children develop—of themselves and others—become the basis for their perspective on life.

I met a man last year who lived most of his adult life trying to become financially prosperous. Everything was sacrificed—family, friends, community. I asked why, and he said, "Because my father predicted that I would never amount to anything, and I wanted to prove him wrong."

"Did you change his mind?" I inquired.

"I'll never know," the man replied. "He's been dead for ten years."

This man's father had staked his claim to authority by cursing rather than blessing his son. "First, do no harm," the philosopher/doctor Hippocrates warned. That should be our guideline. We call out, plead, implore, but in the end we must bless and not curse.

If I pass the baton as best I can, then I can live with a clear conscience. We shouldn't really take responsibility for more than that.

Passing the baton as best I can, however, entails an enormous amount of responsibility. Perhaps as you read through this chapter it occurred to you that it might not be good if a younger person closely followed your example. This is a tough one: what if I'm not sure my example is worth following? How persistent should I be in passing the baton if I've had failure in my life?

Mary Poppins was Wrong: How to Make Your Mess Your Message

"But you, chosen generation, you weak things of the world, who have forsaken all, that ye may follow the Lord; go after Him, and confound the mighty; go after Him, ye beautiful feet, and shine ye in the firmament . . . . He whom you cleave unto, is exalted, and hath exalted you. Run ye to and fro, and be known unto all nations."

St. Augustine

"WHO AM I TO CALL ANOTHER PERSON TO A BETTER LIFE? I SHOULD TALK. LOOK AT ME! WHO WOULD LISTEN?"

Perhaps more than any other factor, my deep-seated guilt about not having fulfilled my own potential is the thing that keeps me from calling the next generation to a higher standard.

THE MARY POPPINS LIFE

You may recall the clever scene in the movie "Mary Poppins" in which she, as a new nanny, reveals her measuring tape to the children she'll be caring for.

This unusual device measures character, not height. Much to the children's horror, it accurately identifies their flaws. After viewing their own results, the children insist that Mary measure herself. She does so and reads the description, clucking, "Just as I thought. 'Mary Poppins: Practically perfect in every way.'"

At this very moment I'm rolling my eyes at Mary Poppins. Sure, I want to improve myself. But to be perfect? It can't happen! I don't even want to try!

Furthermore, I'm filled with suspicion of anyone who does seem to be perfect. I ask myself, "What is he hiding?"

Young adults certainly think this way. One student told me, "I want to find someone who can mentor me, but I keep seeing the failure in the lives of older adults. I try, but I just can't respect them."

Another student who had grown up in the inner city told me that the people and institutions that should have shown him a better way actually cut him adrift. "I saw my father in church saying 'Bless God' and lifting his hands, but I know what drugs he smoked that morning before church. And then I looked around at the leaders in the church. Deacon 'X' is sleeping with 'Y' in the choir, the son of Pastor 'Z' has a sideline business in grand theft auto, and so on. Who could I turn to?"

If we can't lead by example, how can we lead?

But God does not let us off so easily. Second Timothy 3:16-17 says,

> All scripture is given by inspiration of God, and is profitable for doctrine, for reproof, for correction, for instruction in righteousness: That the man of God may be *perfect* (emphasis mine), thoroughly furnished unto all good works (KJV).

Translations of that word "perfect" are so varied that it's confusing to most people. One scholar translates it as "complete." Another translates it as "adequate."

Perfect? Complete? *Adequate*?

When three different words are used to describe something, there's only one thing to do: look back at the original Greek word the Apostle Paul used.

The three most commonly used words for "perfect" in the New Testament are these:

- *teleios* (complete in character, grown up)
- *katartizo* (to restore to its original condition)
- *artios* (to freshen up, lifted, loosened)

Paul uses the word "artios" here. The root word "arti" is derived from "airo" and means "to suspend." The word "perfect" here comes from the same root word as our word "airplane." It implies lifting-up, loosing from the bonds of something, being cleaned-up from dirtiness.

The Greeks didn't have a concept of flying contraptions, obviously, but they may have used the word "airo" to describe the "lifting up" of an anchor so that a ship can be free to sail.

This is a profound breakthrough for me. All of my life I thought that the Bible and church were for the purpose of nailing me down . . . keeping me from floating away. That's why I had to come back every week—because I came loose and had to be nailed down again.

But the exact *opposite* is actually the case. The measure of my spiritual maturity is not whether others see me as flawless, but whether they see that, with a standard of truth based in God's Word, I am setting sail in my God-given design and purpose.

John A. Shedd, the Chicago department store magnate (and the man after whom Chicago's Shedd Aquarium is named) said, "A ship in the harbor is safe. But that is not what ships are for." Isn't it time to lift the anchors and venture out?

MARY POPPINS DIDN'T HAVE A STORY THIS GOOD

What this generation needs is a model of persistence, not perfection. Claims of perfection are suspicious, but persistent action is almost universally admired. Don't pretend to be something you're not—just set the pace for doing what is right.

Because most of us are somewhere in this journey, we assume that we can't use our lives as an example for those to whom we're passing the baton. But that's the whole point: you're a little farther down the road, and can impart wisdom through both your successes and your failures.

So, if you've let yourself be sidetracked in the pursuit of your dream, tell the story. If you gave up your dream for a time to accomplish some honorable task, talk about the character you developed in making that decision.

As a mentor of mine regularly points out, "Your mess is your message." Tell the whole story and inspire those who come behind to live out their God-given design. Whether it's hard or easy, discovering your calling is an essential part of passing the baton.

TURNING YOUR GIFTS INTO INFLUENCE

One of the great myths about mentoring—or discipleship or whatever you want to call it—is that you must reproduce yourself in the ones you mentor. This discourages most of us. "If they really knew me, they wouldn't want to have my image in them." In reality, your goal isn't to reproduce yourself in them, but to help them to be everything God designed them to be.

Ask yourself:

- What did others do to invest meaningfully in my life?
- How do I *wish* someone had invested in my life?
- How do I naturally like to spend time with other people?
- What important realities do I think others ought to know?
- What do I wish I had known at a younger age?

Then find opportunities to pass this information along to the next generation.

The best influencers, the ones who will leave an indelible impression on the next generation, are those who mentor and coach and sponsor *according to their bent*. They live as close to 100% of their gifts as they can, and they seek to encourage their protégés to do the same.

Even as I suggest this, however, I know what the big obstacle is. In this postmodern age, the younger generation has been taught that truth is different for each person. I can see it now: you try to build into someone's life and he says, "That's so nice. I'm glad that it worked for you. But the times are different."

What will you say when that happens?

Shutting Up: How to Stop Giving Advice and Start Having an Influence

"He that takes truth for his guide, and duty for his end, may safely trust to God's providence to lead him aright."
Blaise Pascal

My neighbor, Bob, wants to make a difference. He loves writing letters and going to meetings. He's in his early 60s and knows ten times as much about computers as I do, as well as how to use the Internet to strategic political advantage.

Bob knows a *lot* about what is going on in America, and he's happy to hold forth to those willing to listen. Some time ago I ambled over to visit Bob in his office—more specifically, half of a garage workshop converted into a high-tech information center with banks of computers, two satellite dishes, a refrigerator full of diet soda, and a few stray animals.

"Jeff," he said in frustration the moment I arrived, "the thing that drives me up the wall

about young people today is that they are so
polite."

"And . . . that's . . . bad?" I asked, waiting for
the punch line.

"They don't listen at *all*," Bob continued. "I
try to tell them what's really going on, and they
respectfully nod their heads and say, 'Hmmm,'
but they turn around and walk away and think
I'm nuts."

He's right, you know. Garrison Keillor said,
"You taught me to be nice, so nice that now I am
so full of niceness, I have no sense of right and
wrong, no outrage, no passion." In the face of
evil and injustice, niceness is no virtue.

But what is to be done? How can we
influence the "nice" people who don't want to
hear it? The answer is simultaneously simple
and complex: to light the match of those in the
next generation, I can't just *tell* them the truth, I
must *show* it to them. Here are three quick ways
to do that:

1. ASK PERMISSION

Think of truth as a flashlight. If someone shines a flashlight in your face, it's confrontational—even threatening. Your defenses go up. But if a person points the flashlight beam down the rocky trail you'll be treading, you feel relief and gratefulness.

Convince others of the truth not by *explaining* the truth, but by *showing what difference it makes to embrace the truth*. Here are some simple conversation openers:

- May I tell you about a personal experience that might make the way clearer for you?
- Can I share something with you in a spirit of love?
- I've had an experience that might shed some light on your current situation, and I'd be happy to share it if you're interested.
- I know of another way that might work. Would you like to hear it?

2. FOLLOW UP CONSISTENTLY

John Stonestreet, one of the young men I've had the privilege to mentor, is Executive Director for Summit Ministries. He's also a successful mentor in his own right. John once told me, "It's pretty simple to mentor kids. I just stop them in the hall and ask a couple of questions about how things are going. A few days later I follow up to see how they're doing. It shows them that I'm open to talking about what concerns them."

This direct approach to mentoring is especially important for teachers. Earlier I noted that only about 5% of young people see their teachers as having credible insight into the important issues in life. Kids tend to see teachers as people who *tell*, not *ask*, so they don't ask or tell their teachers anything important.

Yet 55% of teens say that they are most likely to seek advice from their friends. Is it because their friends tell them what they want to hear? Perhaps. But more likely, it's because their friends will listen and ask questions in a non-threatening way.

Please understand: I'm not suggesting that there's no place for confrontation. But most people already know they fall short. What they need is encouragement—literally, someone to give them the courage—to do what they know is right.

My friend Gina told me that her late father did that for her by habitually asking his children, "What are your dreams, goals, and aspirations?"

"I got so tired of it," Gina said, smiling, "but I could never get away from it. I knew he cared, and that he would always encourage me and support me to live a better life."

3. ANSWER A QUESTION WITH A QUESTION

One of my mentors bluntly told me, "Jeff, because you're a teacher, you assume that you have to teach in order for other people to learn. You're wrong."

I hate to admit it, but my mentor was right. I once went to hear a speaker who was addressing a complex political problem. He was so articulate that I found myself thinking, "I'm glad he's got my back on that issue. Now I don't have to think about it anymore."

Whoa. Hold on a sec. If that speaker is to be truly successful, he can't just demonstrate that he knows what he is talking about. He needs to move *me* to action. Otherwise, my complacency will grow in direct proportion to his expertise.

The same is true in one-on-one mentoring relationships. If the one I am mentoring believes that I can solve all his problems, then he stops thinking for himself and becomes passive. This is a bad outcome. After all, the point of passing the baton is that they can *go somewhere* with it.

My real purpose should be to *unleash* the person, not create dependency.

So...how do we actually unleash people? Let's take an in-depth look at that question in the next chapter.

Fourteen Questions to Unleash the Potential of Those You Influence

"A prudent question is one-half of wisdom."
Francis Bacon

As a novice professor I had students coming to my office at all hours and accosting me in the hall. They wanted my solution for this or that problem, and I was happy to comply. Frankly, I felt needed, and was glad that people liked what I had to say. After several weeks of this bombardment, however, I started dreading encounters with my students.

In desperation I began writing down questions that I could ask to help students solve their own problems. These questions aren't unique, but perhaps you'll find them helpful in unlocking the thought processes of those you're mentoring, enhancing their problem-solving ability, and even lowering defensiveness.

The question-asking conversation usually begins with a check-in:

- "What is going on with 'X'?"
- "Is this a good time to talk about 'Y'?"
- "I've been thinking about your work on 'Z' and wanted to see if there are any ways I can support you."

My goal in asking these questions is not to look for an opportunity to give instruction, but to help my students solve problems for themselves.

- "What do you think about that?"
- "Why is that happening?"
- "What took place?"
- *"What would you like to see happen?"*

That last question, *"What would you like to see happen?"* is a bit strange, so let me explain it. It's essentially the question Jesus asked when a blind man called out to him, "Lord, have mercy on me!"

Jesus asked, "What do you want me to do for you?"

I'm sure the disciples were thinking, "Well, duh, Jesus. What do you *think* he wants you to do for him?"

Why did Jesus ask the question when the answer seemed so obvious? *Because some people don't want to have their problems solved.* Some folks have wrapped their identities around their problems. If you solve the problems, their identities disappear. That's why if you solve one problem for them, they'll immediately come up with another.

If you ask someone, "What do you want to see happen?" and they say "Nothing," you can reply, "That's fine. But if there is a way I can support you, let me know."

Sometimes, as in work situations, we don't have the luxury of waiting until the person wants the solution. It's perfectly appropriate to say, "I have a thought about that, but it seems that you are unwilling to hear it. Am I misjudging the situation?"

DON'T SOLVE PROBLEMS

If it turns out that my students genuinely want to change, I still don't give answers. Instead, I ask, "What do you think you need to do?" Usually they know exactly what needs to be done, but they just need to hear it from someone else.

Occasionally a student's solution is wrong, even tragically so. In one such situation I remember thinking, "If you do that, you're going to burn every bridge you've ever built." At this point, for me, there is a *huge* temptation to jump in and start giving advice. Instead, I've learned to ask, "Why do you think that is the appropriate response?" or "What assumptions are you making?" or "What does God say about this?"

Some years ago I received my first invitation to speak at a Fortune 500 company, a big deal for speakers. I enlisted a "coach" to help me prepare for the event. He asked, "What are you planning to do?"

When I told him I was planning to lay into these guys and be tough on them, he asked, "What assumptions are you making?"

"What do you mean?"

"Why would you assume," he probed, "that these folks are any different from the parents or teachers you're accustomed to speaking to?"

My coach was absolutely right. If I had gone in there with both guns blazing, I would have alienated my audience and defeated my purpose for being there. Instead, I spoke to that corporate group just as I would have any church group, without quoting Scripture, of course. It went great and led to future invitations.

Once my students establish a plan of action, I start asking questions like these:

- "Who are the people who can help you with this?"
- "How do you get to them?"
- "When will you act?"

And when it seems like they've got a good plan for getting wise counsel from others, I ask,

- "What barriers do you face?"

I've found that this simple question makes it easier to bring up the reality of the situation. For example, if a student tried to solve this problem before and ran into a brick wall, then the brick wall *is* the problem. Simply having new motivation is not the answer; we have to find ways to knock down those barriers.

At long last, I get around to asking how I can help. I ask questions like these:

- How can I support you?
- What resources do you need?
- How is my feedback helping you?

In my experience, as I ask the questions, follow up, and trust God for the outcome, the truth starts to emerge. As Proverbs 4:18 (ESV), "But the path of the righteous is like the light of dawn, which shines brighter and brighter until full day."

There's one more topic we need to cover, one more barrier that prevents people from influencing the next generation: the fear of failure. What if I invest my life in people and they crash and burn, or, even worse, turn their backs on the truth? What if I pass the baton... and they drop it?

Confronting Failure: What to Do When the Next Generation Blows It

> "Life, like war, is a series of mistakes, and he is not the best Christian nor the best general who makes the fewest false steps. Poor mediocrity may secure that; but he is the best who wins the most splendid victories by the retrieval of mistakes. Forget mistakes: organize victory out of mistakes."
>
> F.W. Robertson

IT IS POSSIBLE, MAYBE EVEN LIKELY, THAT THOSE TO WHOM I PASS THE BATON WILL DROP IT. We've all seen this—a great kid gets messed up with drugs, or blows a career opportunity, or abandons his responsibilities.

What are we supposed to do then?

HEART OF STONE, HEART OF FLESH

King Philip's offer was a tremendous opportunity for the young teacher: "Come teach my 13-year-old son. He's an energetic boy, he'll make a terrific student, and it will be your opportunity to influence a future king. I'll provide everything you need, and every luxury you can imagine."

The teacher set sail for Macedonia immediately. The king was right: his precocious son *was* a fast learner in whatever the teacher placed before him—philosophy, music, science, and politics. Especially politics.

The boy listened carefully as the teacher explained his novel theory about kingship. It's not about the number of people you lead, the teacher told him. Leaders of nations differ from city leaders in *pedigree*, not just degree of responsibility. Royal leaders are a different breed. They're special.

Special, indeed. This the boy willingly believed, but not for reasons anyone could suspect. He had heard rumors, and believed them in his heart, that he was a demi-god, the offspring of his mother Olympia and Zeus. The whole world would someday see just how special he was.

Seven years later, King Philip died under mysterious circumstances and the boy, now age 20, became king. Almost immediately he embarked on a campaign of world domination earning the nickname—through both fear and adoration—Alexander the Great.

Distressed by reports of his pupil's recklessness, the teacher wondered: "Where did I go wrong? Why didn't those lessons on moral goodness and citizenship penetrate Alexander's heart?"

Alexander, too, reflected often on his education, but not in the way the teacher had hoped. He meticulously catalogued and forwarded unusual plant specimens gleaned from each of his conquests. But each time the teacher received one of these gifts, his heart fell. It wasn't *specimens* that he craved; he longed for Alexander's heart of stone to become a heart of flesh.

Within 12 years of becoming king, Alexander the Great was dead. But his legacy lived on—

both in military conquest and in the broken heart of his teacher, Aristotle, the man who became a great philosopher but couldn't reach the heart of his most famous pupil.

A LEADER'S SCARS

Protégés turn against mentors. Children become prodigals. Students rebel against teachers. Heartbreak is a distinct possibility in passing the baton to the next generation.

Such heartbreak scars the soul. These aren't run-of-the-mill scars, the kind you show to your friends. They keep hurting and you want to keep them to yourself.

Some time ago I had the experience of being deeply wounded by someone I had trained. As I was going through that experience I had an empathetic conversation with a horse rancher from Texas: "You know, there's a funny thing about stallions in the wild," he said. "Their bodies are often deeply scarred."

"Why is that?" I asked. "Wild animal attacks?"

He shook his head. "No, they're viciously kicked by the mares under their protection."

All leaders carry scars, received from followers who didn't understand that the leader was acting in their best interests, even though it didn't feel like it at the time.

Maybe you've seen kids in your neighborhood grow up, full of potential, only to take a wrong turn and fall headlong into disaster. A few years ago I received a tearful letter from Victoria, documenting a life filled with regret. She wrote,

> I was one of those children other parents warned their kids to stay away from. I did drugs, was promiscuous, thought nothing of breaking the law if I felt like it, yet my parents believed for many years (until the police gave them a dose of reality) that I was a perfect angel who could do no wrong. How

did I manage this? Very easily, really. I lied. Repeatedly and convincingly.

Now Victoria is a single mother of four, experiencing herself the very thing she put her parents through.

It isn't just kids who will break your heart. Anyone you seek to influence might cause pain, whether a student, an employee, or just someone you try to assist in a tough situation.

Jesus had these scars. For three years he invited others to walk with him through life. He prayed for them. He mentored them. He pursued them when they went astray. He wooed them like a bridegroom woos a bride. He challenged them to live worthy of the calling they had received.

But just hours before his death, Jesus turned to one of his disciples and said, "One of you will betray me." This disciple, caught red-handed, left the room. Jesus said to another, "I tell you the truth. This very night, before the rooster crows, you will disown me three times." This disciple was shocked and swore that such a thing was not possible. But by morning, the truth was known. Peter denied his Lord with curses, and all of the other disciples fled.

None of this took Jesus by surprise. For three years he had told story after story about prodigal children, rebellious servants, lost sheep, lost coins. The point of every story was the same: in spite of the pain, it's always worth it to seek and to find that which is lost. Ultimately, he gave his life to do just that.

How could he do this? I'm quite certain the answer will surprise you.

How to Conquer Worry and Fear by Surrendering the Outcome to God

"The greatness of a man's power is the measure of his surrender."

William Booth

I've often wondered where Jesus got the patience and perspective to put up with all of the guff his followers gave him. The answer that appears in Scripture is so simple that I rejected it out of hand the first time I heard it.

Jesus surrendered the outcome to God.

To surrender the outcome to God means acting faithfully through the *process*, but relinquishing control of the *results*.

My goal in passing the baton is to make sure the pass takes place and then cheer my followers on. If I do this faithfully, then I can release any worry about whether the person I hand off to wins the race.

As long as I feel responsible for the outcome of the lives of others, I live in worry. I fret about whether my kids will turn out all right. I wonder whether my students will pass my class. I agonize about having enough money to make payroll in our organization.

But when I surrender the outcome to God, fear melts away. If I'm confident that God will bring about the outcome that pleases him, I'm free to stop wheedling and manipulating and cajoling. I'm free to let God open the floodgates of blessing if he chooses to do so.

A person who rests in God's power alone is said to be "meek." Look up "meekness" in a thesaurus and you'll get the entirely wrong idea: "docile" and "weak-kneed" are some of the synonyms.

Jesus was meek, but he was no sissy. Even faced with his own crucifixion, he knew that God would use whatever happened to bring about the outcome he desired. That's why Jesus was able to pray, though in great agony, "Not my will, but yours be done."

Jesus became little so that the entire world could see—and receive life from—his greatness. Yet it was in meekness that Jesus invested in everyone around him, even those he knew would never change.

Meekness takes a tremendous amount of power, but where does the power come from? Hard work? Cleverness? Self-awareness?

Actually, none of the above. The power to be meek comes from a deep understanding of my own position before God.

Here are some things I've found helpful in surrendering the outcome to God:

See my investment in others in light of eternity. If one of my children rejects the baton pass and makes bad life decisions, I may feel that my own reputation has been damaged. I might respond in fury, "Don't you realize what this does to *me*?" or "*I* thought *I* raised you better than that!"

But if I see my influence in the light of eternity, my response can be, "My goal is to help restore you to the place where your life brings glory to God." When that happens, I rejoice, like the father running out to embrace the prodigal son. When it doesn't happen, I am forced to my knees in humble reliance on God, who works all things together for His good.

Patiently await long-term results. Those who make the greatest difference are those who continue to invest without the expectation of immediate return.

When I started saving toward retirement, my financial counselor advised me to think long term—"Don't even pay attention to daily stock market returns," he said. "All we care about is that the daily gains and losses add up to a substantial rate of growth over 45 years. It's not what happens one day from now, or even ten or a hundred. We care about what the fund will be like in 15,330 days when you're 65 and ready to move into the next season of life."

We all know stories of those who went through prolonged dark seasons only to emerge in the light after what seemed like forever. Maybe this is your own story. Have faith that this will be the next generation's story as well. Let God take responsibility for the outcome of the race, and just pass the baton as best you can.

Put tools in the toolbox, even if they don't care. I'm involved with one of the Summit Ministries camps for high school and college students. At a recent conference a speaker addressed the topic of "Economics from a Biblical Perspective." He was attempting to pass the baton to them, and they were looking at him like he was a Martian. In spite of being a compelling instructor, most of his material went right over the kids' heads. But that's okay; they may not care about economics right now, but when they *do* care—when they have a job and savings account—they'll be able to call to mind what they learned and reference it in their notebook.

It's humbling to hand out shiny new tools only to have the next generation respond, "What the heck? Why do I need *this* in my toolbox?" True, some of the tools you place will never get used. They'll languish in toolboxes all over the world. But have faith that someday, somewhere, those you've influenced will rummage around the toolbox, pull out the now tarnished instrument you gave them, and begin using it.

The same is true in passing the baton. Just pass it as well as you possibly can, starting now. If they fall down, help them up. If they drop it, help them pick it up. *But don't blame yourself.* Surrender the outcome to God and let him bring about the result he desires.

The results God brings about are always more than we can imagine from our limited perspectives. As we shall see, it's like the power of compound interest, but better. It starts slow but accelerates into an unstoppable force.

Compound Influence: The Secret to an Enduring Legacy

"Knowing that we are fulfilling God's purpose is the only thing that really gives rest to the restless human heart."

Chuck Colson

SHORTLY BEFORE HE DIED, THE APOSTLE PAUL WROTE A LETTER TO PASS THE BATON TO TIMOTHY, A YOUNG MAN HE HAD MENTORED FOR YEARS. Here's what he said:

> You then, my child, be strengthened by the grace that is in Christ Jesus, [2] and what you have heard from me in the presence of many witnesses entrust to faithful men who will be able to teach others also. (2 Tim. 2:1-2, ESV).

Notice that there are four generations listed: Paul, Timothy, "Reliable men," and "Others."

Those who influence to the fourth generation can cement their influence for centuries. This is true for evil as well as for good. "I the Lord your

God am a jealous God, visiting the iniquity of the fathers on the children to the third and the fourth generation of those who hate me" (Exodus 20:5 ESV).

Some years ago I began teaching a leadership class for people going into youth ministry. Wanting to encourage them toward good stewardship, I developed a lecture entitled "How to Become a Millionaire on a Youth Pastor's Salary." No one *ever* missed that class period.

It's a pretty simple idea, really. I demonstrated how saving 10% of a low ministry salary starting at age 23 could give you more than a million and a half dollars in a retirement fund.

Then, just so they could see the power of compound interest over four generations, I asked my students to guess how much money would be in that fund if it were left untouched during their lifetime, their child's lifetime, their grandchild's lifetime, and opened only upon the death of their great grandchild.

It's over six *billion* dollars.

That's the power of persistent financial investment of a small amount of money over four generations. And it's just money—it's going to burn, and you can't take it with you.

What would be the cultural—not to mention spiritual—influence if you trained one person to be a trainer of trainers? It's just four people deep. Yet the impact is exponential—to the power of four.

FROM SHOE CLERK TO GLOBAL EVANGELISM

One of my favorite stories about the power of influencing others across generations is that of Edward Kimball, a Boston Sunday school teacher in the 1850s. Working with young men, he placed a lot of tools in a lot of toolboxes. Many of those boys probably never bothered to pull them out.

But one boy did. He was a shoe clerk named D. L. Moody. Twenty-one years later, Moody became America's most well-known evangelist.

On one of his trips, Moody helped spark a spiritual awakening in London. A local pastor, F. B. Meyer, was inflamed with evangelistic zeal, and began placing tools in toolboxes. Preaching in America some years later, Meyer had a transforming influence on a student named J. Wilbur Chapman.

Chapman became involved with the YMCA, which as a strongly Christian organization at the time was a terrific way to put tools in toolboxes. Through the YMCA, Chapman discipled a former pro baseball player named Billy Sunday.

Sunday traveled all across America preaching evangelistic crusades—handing out tools, so to speak. One crusade was organized by a group of North Carolina businessmen, who, pleased with the crusade's success, scheduled another one the following year with Mordecai Hamm as the evangelist. Hamm preached for three weeks. During one of the services, a lanky country boy came forward and gave his life to Christ.

That boy was Billy Graham who, during his decades of preaching, shared the gospel with two billion people.

Everybody's heard of Billy Graham. Lots of people have heard of Billy Sunday and D. L. Moody. But almost no one has heard of Edward Kimball, the humble man whose faithful discipleship of boys has changed the world.

If Edward Kimball had not faithfully placed tools in toolboxes, imagine how the world would have been different.

FAITHFULNESS, NOT FAME

More than two millennia ago the prophet Ezekiel cried out, "[I] sought for a man among them who should build up the wall and stand in the breach before me for the land, that I should not destroy it, but I found none" Ezekiel 22:30 (ESV).

This generation desperately needs people to risk heartbreak and stand in the gap for them. Will you be there?

Shortly before his martyr's death at the hands of Adolf Hitler, German pastor Dietrich Bonhoeffer asked a penetrating question:

> Who stands fast? Only the man whose final standard is not his reason, his principles, his conscience, his freedom, or his virtue, but who is ready to sacrifice all this when he is called to obedient and responsible action in faith and in exclusive allegiance to God—the responsible man who tries to make his whole life an answer to the question and call of God. Where are these responsible people?[21]

With all of my heart, I want to raise my hand and call out, "I'm right here!" I can't say that I know the outcome, or that I'm without fear. But I can trust the one who said, "Those who sow in tears will reap with joy."

The Power of Four starts with you. You're number one. Find a number two and start passing that baton. As you do, maybe you'll take inspiration from one of the best losers in Olympic history. I'll share his story next.

The Final Secret to Finishing Strong in the Race of Life

"I ran and ran every day, and I acquired a sense of determination, this sense of spirit that I would never, never, give up, no matter what else happened."
Wilma Rudolph, the first American woman to win three gold medals in track and field during a single Olympic games, despite running on a sprained ankle

BUD GREENSPAN IS THE GUY WHO MAKES OLYMPIC MOVIES—the thrill of victory, the agony of defeat, and all that. His favorite stories are recorded in a book called *100 Greatest Olympic Moments*. Most of the stories are of Olympic winners, but at least one is of the best loser I've ever heard of.

John Stephen Akwari traveled from Tanzania to run the marathon in the Mexico City Olympics in 1968. During the race he fell down and was injured, yet he stood up, allowed a bandage to be applied, and limped toward the finish line.

Akwari moved so slowly that he didn't make it back to the stadium until an hour after the race had concluded. As he made his way around the track for a final lap, word swept through the crowd: "This is the last man in the marathon. He didn't give up!" A slow rhythmic clapping sound began to resound throughout the stadium. When Akwari crossed the finish line, the place erupted. One commentator said that the crowd was so enthusiastic that you could have sworn that Akwari had just won the gold medal.

After the race, reporters peppered Akwari with questions: "Why didn't you just quit?"

He replied, "I don't think you understand. My country did not send me to Mexico City to start the race. My country sent me to *finish* the race."[22]

You and I were not sent here to start the race, but to run our lap flat out—to leave it all on the track. Furthermore, our finishing of the race gives meaning to all of those who have run before.

Hebrews chapter 11 in the Bible is called the "Hall of Faith" because it celebrates great men and women of faith. It tells of great deeds, of horrible tortures, all endured out of faith. But the chapter concludes with a startling passage:

> And all these, though commended through their faith, did not receive what was promised, since God had provided something better for us, that apart from us they should not be made perfect (Hebrews 11:39-40, ESV).

Do you mean to tell me that Noah's life takes on more meaning because of how I live mine? Yes. That Abraham and Sarah and all of the martyrs—their sacrifices make more sense in light of how I act now? Absolutely. What follows that passage is even more astounding:

> Therefore, since we are surrounded by so great a cloud of witnesses, let us also lay aside every weight, and sin which clings so closely, and let us run with endurance the

race that is set before us . . . (Hebrews 12:1 ESV).

Can you imagine it? All of the great heroes of the faith are counting on *you*. They're cheering for *you*!

Can you hear them? Noah's up there hollering, "Hey! Don't give up! You're almost to the finish line! Keep running! I built a boat for 100 years, and I didn't even know what rain was! You can do this!"

Maybe Abraham is up there too. "Don't quit!" he yells from the stands. "You have no idea how old my wife and I were when we had that kid! Nothing is impossible with God! Keep running!"

The voices come from all quarters. A great cloud of witnesses, all on their feet, watching as you enter the stadium for your final lap. At this point it doesn't matter if you have fallen down. It doesn't matter if you're bruised and bloodied and covered in sweat. Pass the baton!

Very soon the race will be over and you'll fall across that finish line into the arms of your coach. Don't you long to hear him say, "Well done, good and faithful servant! Enter into my joy"?

Your life is significant in the light of all of the other saints who have lived. It is your destiny to take your place at the finish line with all of the truly greats. There are no "also rans" in this life.

I told you earlier about the story of Pa Dan. What I did not tell you is that at the very end of his life, at age 90, he told my grandmother, "Well, I've given my life to Jesus and told him he can do whatever he wants with my life." Pa Dan fell down, but he crossed the finish line. What he longed to hear was put into song by my brother Scott, a worship pastor:

There will come a day when the words have all been spoken,
And we understand what remains and what is broken;
Then we shall see Him as He is.

I do not fear the flame, for my pardon has been granted,
Sealed by sovereign grace, though I'll never understand it;
Though still I long to finish well.

So I will run this race, knowing I'll see Your face.
And I will seize this day, longing to hear You say:

Well done! My good and faithful servant;
Enter my glory—I've been waiting for you!
Well run!
The course I set before you was never meant to be an easy one.

Well done!

We must fix our eyes on the shining face of Jesus,
And listen for the crowd that surrounds us and sees us;
Heaven's heroes finish strong!

So will you run this race, knowing you'll see his face?

So will you seize this day, longing to hear him say:

Well done! My good and faithful servant;
Enter my glory—I've been waiting for you!
Well run!
The course I set before you was never meant to be an easy one.
Well done!"[23]

("Well Done" by Scott Myers
On "Quench My Thirst")

That's our challenge, and that is what makes life count—that we are faithful, that we run the race, and that, by God's grace, we finish well.

So we return to the question posed at the beginning of this book. We're rounding the last curve in the track. The next generation glances our way in hope and expectation, hand outstretched, poised to burst into the sprint of life. Will we as a generation make the pass? Will *you* make the pass? What will the story of our generation be? The answer, quite literally, is in your hands.

What On Earth Do We Do Now?

"Nobody made a greater mistake than he who did
nothing because he could do only a little."

Edmund Burke

Two years ago the concern over what will
happen to the next generation led to the
formation of *Passing the Baton International*
(PTBI), a non-profit organization dedicated to
shifting the paradigm of how we train the next
generation. The goal of PTBI is to mobilize one
million adults worldwide who will take personal
responsibility to mentor, coach and disciple the
next generation of culture-shaping leaders.

Here are some ways to participate in this great
cause. Some are simple, some require greater
commitment. Questions? Contact me personally
at jeff@passingthebaton.org or 423-570-1000.

1. **Stay in touch!** I send a free weekly e-mail
   newsletter called *Get Ready to Lead*. I'll alert
   you to trends and helpful tips and techniques
   for reaching the hearts of the next

generation. Sign up at
www.passingthebaton.org.

2. **Order more copies of *Handoff* to
distribute to your friends.** Go to
www.handoffbook.com to get more copies
of this book. The best recommendations *of*
this book are from those who have read the
words *in* this book!

3. **Bring this cause of Passing the Baton
to the attention of lots of people.**
Christianity is always only one generation
away from extinction. It's scary, but also
exciting when we realize that what we do
actually makes a difference. I want to help
you get the word out to your group. If you
order 500 copies of this book I'll come
speak to your group for <u>free</u>—I'll even pay
my own expenses. Consider the ways this
could serve you:

- It could generate excitement for a special
church service.
- It could provide a nice table gift at a
fundraising banquet.

- It could be a gift for parents or grads at a commencement.
- It could be an incentive to sign up for a conference.
- It could serve as a premium to encourage donations to a worthy non-profit group.

This offer applies only in the U.S. and Canada, and only a limited number of dates are available. You can e-mail me directly at jeff@passingthebaton.org and I'll pass the information on to our event planner.

4. **Invest three days to transform the rest of your life.** Each year I host a three day strategic planning/visioneering/mission-building/encouraging workshop called *Wisdom Trek*. Along with certified life coaches who work with you one-on-one during the conference and afterward, I show you how to craft a life-long plan to unleash your gifts and break through the barriers

that stop you from succeeding. Go to
www.passingthebaton.org for more info.

5. **Spark new life in your group by mobilizing those around you to joyfully invest in the next generation.** In the last two years close to 400 organizations have benefited from the six-hour *Passing the Baton* workshop that focuses on mobilizing attendees to mentor, coach and disciple the next generation of leaders. Studies show that workshop graduates are significantly more likely to feel comfortable, willing and prepared to mentor and coach others. Go to www.passingthebaton.org for information on booking this workshop.

6. **Call out and train some young adults with our easy-to-use resources.** Through an arrangement with B & H Publishers I've produced three leadership courses. In six DVD lessons *Secrets of the World Changers* shows how to discover your mission in life and set goals to

accomplish it. *Secrets of Great Communicators* includes six DVD lessons to help you prepare and confidently deliver a speech. *Secrets of Everyday Leaders* is a 12-part DVD course that shows you how to break down the 12 most common barriers leaders face. Each kit contains a study guide, DVD and a CD-ROM with lesson plans. If you can push the "play" button on a DVD player, you can train leaders. For more information go to www.passingthebaton.

7. **Become a conversational leader.** The only viable leaders of the future will be those who lead by growing the leaders around them. We call it "leader development" or "leadership coaching." In association with the Center for the Advancement of Christian Coaching, PTBI offers an eight-week course that extends your everyday influence as a leader through the dynamics of professional coaching. You'll spend two days "in person" with our coach trainer and then receive eight weeks of distance training and coaching in the art

of developing your followers. You'll learn how to reduce your own crushing workload by skillfully growing others into leaders. You'll find out how to reduce stress by coaching others toward excellence rather than manipulating them into being more "motivated." Studies show that organizations with coaches are four times as likely to reach their goals. Go to www.passingthebaton.org

8. **Sponsor young people into positions of significant influence.** When I was a rebellious 17-year-old an older single lady in our church gave my dad a brochure for a program called Summit Ministries and said, "I think Jeff should go to this." As a result of that conversation I attended Summit's two-week training course in leadership and apologetics. It literally changed my life. Now I'm chairman of the board of that organization and believe that its courses are essential for Christian young people to get their bearings and to prepare to be leaders. Go to www.summit.org.

Endnotes

[1] George Barna, article on www.barna.org.

[2] Ram Charan, "Ending the CEO Succession Crisis, *Harvard Business Review*, February 2005, p. 1.

[3] Ephraim Schwartz, *InfoWorld*, March 6, 2006, p. 12.

[4] Christopher Conte, "Expert Exodus," *Governing*, February 2006.

[5] Mary Grayson, *Hospitals & Health Networks*, November 2005, p. 6.

[6] Jennifer J Salopek, *Training and Development*, June 2005, p. 23.

[7] "Only Half of Protestant Pastors Have a Biblical Worldview,' January 12, 2004. www.barna.org.

[8] George Barna, *Transforming Children into Spiritual Champions* (Ventura, CA: Regal Books, 2003), p. 125.

[9] Dennis Prager, "Baby Boomers Owe America's Young People an Apology," Blog entry for December 4, 2007, www.townhall.com.

[10] Mary Farrar, *Choices: For Women Who Long to Discover Life's Best* (Sisters, OR: Multnomah, 1994), pp. 17-18.

[11] Salopek, p. 23.

[12] Ravi Zacharias, "Reaching the Happy, Thinking Pagan," www.rzim.com, no date provided.

[13] C. John Sommerville, *How the News Makes Us Dumb: The Death of Wisdom in an Information Society* (Downers Grove, IL: InterVarsity, 1999).

[14] George Barna, "A New Generation of Adults Bends Moral and Sexual Rules to Their Liking," October 31, 2006, www.barna.org.

[15] This figure comes from the "Monitoring the Future" Study done each year by the Institute for Social Research at the University of Michigan, which is always worth looking at. Go to www.monitoringthefuture.org.

[16] USA Today, August 19, 2004.

[17] Sarah Hinlickey, "Talking to Generation X," *First Things,* 1999, pp. 10-11.

[18] Lisa Popyk, "Killers Gave Plenty of Warning Signs," *@ The Post: Worldwide Web Edition of the Cincinnati Post,* November 10, 1998.

[19] Gűnther Krallman, *Mentoring for Mission: A Handbook on Leadership Exemplified by Jesus Christ* (Waynesboro, GA: Gabriel, 2003).

[20] Bill Thrall, Bruce McNicol, and Ken McElrath, *The Ascent of a Leader: How Ordinary Relationships Develop Extraordinary Character and Influence* (San Francisco: Jossey-Bass, 1999), p. 52.

[21] Dietrich Bonhoeffer, "After Ten Years." *Letters and Papers from Prison.* Enlarged Edition, Eberhard Bethge, ed. (New York: The Macmillan Company, 1971), p. 5.

[22] Bud Greenspan, *100 Greatest Moments in Olympic History* (Los Angeles: General Publishing Group, Inc., 1995), p. 98.

[23] Scott Myers, on the worship CD entitled *Quench My Thirst*, available at www.passingthebaton.org.